CONSULTANTS & SPONSORS GUIDE TO STABLE VALUE

BY CHRIS TOBE, CFA
WITH KEN TOBE

ISBN-13:
978-1515055341

ISBN-10:
1515055345

TABLE OF CONTENTS

ABOUT THE AUTHOR
ACKNOWLEDGMENTS
INTRODUCTION - STABLE VALUE THE FORGOTTEN ASSET CLASS & HISTORY
CHAPTER 1 - DEFINING STABLE VALUE
CHAPTER 2 - INSURANCE COMPANY GENERAL ACCOUNT - BLAST FROM THE PAST
CHAPTER 3 – INSURANCE COMPANY SEPARATE ACCOUNT- SMOKE AND MIRRORS
CHAPTER 4 - SYNTHETIC GIC'S OR WRAPS
CHAPTER 5 - POOLED FUNDS OR COLLECTIVE INVESTMENT TRUSTS
CHAPTER 6 - CONSULTAN T & PLAN SPONSOR PERSPECTIVES
CHAPTER 7 - BENCHMARKING & PERFORMANCE
CHAPTER 8- FIXED INCOME UNDERLYING INVESTMENTS
CHAPTER 9 - RISKS, DEFINED
CHAPTER 10 - RISK APPLICATIONS
CHAPTER 11 - REGULATORY & LEGAL
CHAPTER 12 - SYNTHETIC GIC OPERATING RISKS
CHAPTER 13 - FEES
CHAPTER 14 COMEBACK & FUTURE
APPENDIX

ABOUT THE AUTHOR

Chris Tobe founded Stable Value Consultants in 2009. He and his wife Lisa Scott Tobe a Neurosurgery Nurse Practitioner at the University of Louisville Trauma Center together have 6 children and reside in Anchorage, Kentucky.

Chris Tobe, CFA, CAIA has been a nationally known expert in Stable Value for over 15 years, with institutional investment experience of over 26 years. Stable Value Consultants is a niche firm that will do project, hourly, and retainer consulting for plans, collective trusts and the stable value industry along with expert witness work. The firm is set up to help plans minimize their liability in their stable value option, by evaluating and doing due diligence on the current portfolio, or by assisting in searches and transitions. With SVC he consulted to seven separate Stable Value clients with 23 different stable value pools ranging in size from $100 million to $10 billion including stable value projects for two large public plans Texas and Maryland and several large corporate plans and collective trusts. Tobe has worked recently with a number of large DC plans and has been quoted in the Wall Street Journal and Barron's on Stable Value. He provided written testimony on stable value to DOL's ERISA advisory committee and testified in person at the joint SEC-DOL hearing on Target Date Funds in summer of 2009.

He has over 25 years of experience working with DC Plans working as a consultant, money manager and regulator. For nearly 7 years he served as a director for the Pension & Savings Group of AEGON Institutional Markets, where he was responsible for a number of major relationships with the over $40 billion wrapped stable value book. Tobe met with DOL officials and authored the AEGON comment letter on the QDIA in 2006.

Tobe has published a number of articles on Stable Value and related topics including "The Consultants Guide to Stable Value," in the Journal of Investment Consulting and "Will the Mutual Fund Scandal Make Equity Washes Easier to Swallow?" in Stable Times. Previous articles include "Stable Value – An Asset for All Seasons" (Plan Sponsor Magazine), "Is Wrapper Capacity a Concern?" (Stable Times), "Rx for Low Cash Yields" (Health Care Financial Management Magazine), and "Enhance multi-employer plans yields" (Employee Benefit Journal). He has served on a number of committees of the Stable Value Investment Association (SVIA) including a stint as the editor of Stable Times magazine. He has spoken at a number of SVIA conferences and national conferences such as IFEBP and NAGDCA on stable value.

He holds a BA in Economics from Tulane University, and an MBA in Finance from Indiana University – Bloomington. He is the past president of the CFA Society of Louisville.

Articles by Chris Tobe:

Is No Stable Value Negligent
http://www.marketwatch.com/story/are-401ks-without-a-stable-value-option-negligent-2014-04-21

<u>Stable Value not Money Market</u>
http://www.marketwatch.com/story/do-money-market-funds-belong-in-401ks-2013-08-30

<u>Measuring Stable Value Risk Structures -- A New Scoring System</u> December 3, 2012
http://papers.ssrn.com/sol3/papers.cfm?abstract_id=2184534

Stable Value Structures
http://www.marketwatch.com/story/how-stable-is-your-stable-value-fund-2012-11-21

<u>Stable Value: Blast to the Past or Too Big to Fail?</u>
Benefits Magazine, Volume 48, No. 12, December 2011, pp. 34-38

<u>NAGDCA SV brochure takes a wrong turn</u> Stable Value Consultants Whitepaper September 2010

<u>Financial Crisis and Subsequent Regulations effect on Stable Value</u> Stable Value Consultants Whitepaper August 2010

Stable Value Insider -Wrap Capacity Back to the Future BCAP Whitepaper April 2010

Support new rules on Investment Fiduciaries in 401(k) Plans   Short Written Testimony submitted to ERISA Advisory Committee March 2010

Stable Value Update Written Testimony submitted to ERISA Advisory Committee October 2009

Target Date Funds Written Testimony SEC-DOL Joint Hearing on Target Date Funds July 2009 http://www.sec.gov/news/press/2009/2009-138.htm

Stable Value Written Testimony submitted to ERISA Advisory Committee June 2009

Spotlight Stable Value- BCAP Consulting Whitepaper published April 2009 commenting on our quotes in the Wall Street Journal, Barrons and CBS Marketwatch.

Mostly Stable Value- BCAP Consulting Whitepaper published February 2009

Stable Value- Weathering the Storm NEPC Whitepaper published 2009 coauthored with Brian Donaghue

Collective Trust Funds Fuel Growth in Stable Value Stable Value Investment Association Newsletter 3rd Quarter 2007 • Volume 11 Issue 3

Editors Corner, Stable Value Investment Association Newsletter 1st Quarter 2007 • Volume 11 Issue 1

Stable Value Excluded from QDIA Based on Faulty Assumptions, Stable Value Investment Association Newsletter 4th Quarter 2006 • Volume 10 Issue 4

Stable Value & Social Security: What Could the Push for Social Security Privatization Mean for Stable Value? Stable Value Investment Association Newsletter 2nd Quarter 2005 • Volume 9 Issue 2

The Consultants Guide to Stable Value by Christopher B. Tobe, CFA the Journal of Investment Consulting Vol.7 No. 1 Summer 2004

Will the Mutual Fund Scandal Make Equity Washes Easier to Swallow? Stable Value Investment Association Newsletter Third Quarter 2004 • Volume 8 Issue 3

Is Wrapper Capacity a Concern? Stable Value Investment Association Newsletter Third Quarter 2003 • Volume 7 Issue 3 Chris Tobe, CFA

Self-Directed Brokerage Accounts Current Trends and Issues – AEGON Institutional Markets White Paper prepared for SVIA Conference – October 2002

Stable Value- Asset for All Seasons Plan Sponsor Magazine July 2002

Speeches by Chris Tobe:

Lexington Employee Benefits Council on Stable Value May 2011

IFEBP Investments Institutes on Stable Value April 2011

Southern Employee Benefits Conference on Stable Value March 2011

IFEBP Nov 2010 Asset Allocation and Assumed Rates of Return

Revere Group Chicago Oct 2010 Stable Value

Target Date Funds NAGDCA WebCast July 2010

Stable Value, GAO conference call presentation March 2010

Stable Value Louisville Employee Benefits Council January 2010 Louisville

Target Date Funds CIEBA January 2010 Washington DC

Fixed Income Indexing & Securities Lending Super Bowl of Indexing December 2009 Phoenix

SEC-DOL Joint Hearing on Target Date Funds Washington DC July 2009

Video at http://www.dol.gov/dol/media/webcast/hearing/

Stable Value Marketing – FRA DCIO conference Boston March 2009

Stable Value in Target Date Funds September 2008 NAGDCA Public DC Conference

www.nagdca.org/documents/Stable_Value_Final.ppt

Health & Welfare Investment Strategies IFEBP Investments Institute, April 2006

Plan Rollover- Stay for the Stable Value IIR GIC Conference April 2005

TIPS in DC plans Stable Value Investment Association (SVIA) Conference October 2004

Under the Hood - Strategies for Stable Value IIR GIC Conference April 2004

Competing Funds SVIA October 2003

Competing Funds IIR GIC Conference April 2003

Self-Directed Brokerage SVIA October 2002

Short term investments and wraps IFEBP Conference Nov 2003

TIPS Stable Value Inv. Assoc. Conference – October 2003

Competing Funds IIR April 2003

TIPS as an Asset Class National Association of State Treasurers RI 2002

Self-Directed Brokerage Accounts Current Trends and Issues Stable Value Inv. Assoc. Conference – October 2002

ACKNOWLEDGEMENTS

For the book production I want to thank my son Ken for his help in writing, editing, website, and production. And lastly, I want to thank my wife Lisa for bringing in the steady paychecks while I put together this book.

INTRODUCTION

STABLE VALUE: THE FORGOTTEN ASSET CLASS

Stable Value is a huge asset class with $719 billion in assets[1] according to the Stable Value Investment Association (SVIA), an industry advocacy group.[2] Stable Value as defined here is confined to United States Defined Contribution retirement plans, primarily 401(k) s, which are the fastest growing part of the U.S. investment market.

Stable value assets have more than tripled since 2000. [3] The growth of the 401(k) market in the U.S. has been incredible; growing from $1.7 trillion in 1995,[4] to $5.9 trillion at the end of 2013. The growth has been especially big with larger 401(k)'s. Mega plans over $500 million in assets which typically have over 5000 employees make up the Aon Hewitt database where stable value has averaged 10% to 20% of assets. According to the Money market directory there are 800 plans of over $500 million in assets. According to Aon Hewitt these largest plans put much more in stable value than all other fixed income bond funds and money market combined. [5]
Considering that many of the several hundred thousand smaller plans do not have Stable Value, Cerulli, in 2014, estimated that stable value products represent 8.9% of all 401(k) assets.

Stable value is a unique conservative asset class providing consistently better returns than money market funds. It is an asset class with low return volatility, protection of principal and interest, and many times low fees.

Stable value options are included in two-thirds of all defined contribution plans. Stable value suffers an identity crisis because a stable value fund option may operate under numerous different names across plans. *Preservation, Income, Guaranteed, GICs, Stable, Principal Protection,* and *Capital Accumulation* are a few of the key words used as stable value fund titles.[6]

HISTORY

Stable value has existed since the invention of the 401(k) in the 1970s. The Evolution of Stable Value as outlined in Handbook of Stable Value (published by Frank Fabozzi in 1998) chronicles traditional Guaranteed Investment Contracts (GIC's) evolving in the 1970 and 1980's. [7]

The section of the Internal Revenue Code that made 401(k) plans possible was enacted into law in 1978.[8] It was intended to allow taxpayers a tax break on deferred income. In 1980, a benefits consultant named Ted Benna took note of the previously obscure provision and figured out it could be used to create a simple, tax-advantaged way to save for retirement.

The stable value industry changed dramatically following three highly publicized insurance company failures in the early 1990s. These insurance company insolvencies raised concerns among plan sponsors on single entity credit risk of traditional GICs, the vehicle predominantly used as the stable value investment in defined contribution plans. The primary concern was credit exposure to the issuer since only the credit of the issuer backs the contract's guarantees. Another major concern was a lack of flexibility and control since assets backing the contract's liabilities are owned and managed by the issuer and the contract is essentially illiquid at the plan level.

Chapter 7 of the Fabozzi Handbook of Stable value by Tami Pease claims the move to synthetics was pushed by the speed that these insurance companies went into bankruptcy. The three specific insolvencies were the Executive Life Seizure in 1991, the Mutual Benefit Life Seizure in 1991-1992 and the Confederation Life Seizure in 1994. Executive Life was rated AAA by S&P until a downgrade to A in February 1990, but in less than a year defaulted on its Guaranteed Investment Contracts (GIC's) in February 1991. [9] Mutual Benefit Life was AAA by S&P until May 1990, and was seized by regulators in July 1991. Confederation Life was AAA until January 1992, and was still A+ until April 1994, but by August of 1994 was seized by regulators. [10]

The insurance industry's first reaction to the insolvencies in the early 90's was the development of "separate account" GIC structures, which segregated the assets backing the contract from the issuer's general account. Assets held in a separate account cannot be used to satisfy general account obligations until the separate account liabilities have been fully satisfied. Having specific assets back the contract alleviated some of the credit concerns around being made whole in the event of insolvency; however, concerns around flexibility and control remained, since the issuer still legally owns the assets in the separate account.

Synthetic GICs were developed to address both sets of concerns. The first Synthetics were introduced by Bankers Trust in 1990. Others soon followed and by 1993 the business started to grow. Synthetics were in full force by the late 90's with the largest 401(k) plans. This structure allows plans to retain legal title to plan assets (thereby reducing credit exposure to any one company or industry) while still delivering the stable value benefits participants have come to expect from traditional GICs. It also allows plan sponsors to exercise greater control over asset selection and investment strategy, and enables greater diversification and safety, potentially higher crediting rates, potentially lower costs, and enhanced control and flexibility when compared to other stable value alternatives, such as traditional or separate account GICs.

By the mid 90's, synthetics were dominant in mega plans over $500 million and had significant exposure to plans $100 to $500 million in assets through collective investment trusts or pools. Stable Value mutual funds were first registered in 1997, but were never a significant part of the market and were shut down by the SEC in 2004. I attribute the shutdown to political pressures put on primarily by the money market industry.[11]

By the mid 2000's synthetic based stable value had a huge share with the largest Fortune 50 type plans and in collective trusts with the fastest growing 401(k) providers like Fidelity, Vanguard and T.Rowe Price. Large mega banks by the mid 2000's had a much larger market share of the synthetic GIC's insuring or covering these plans than large life insurance companies, but this came to an abrupt halt in 2008.

Pre-2008 the banks were providing synthetic GICS at even 4 basis points (4/100 of one percent) far below insurance companies who were providing wrap coverage at around 8 basis points. However, after the 2008 crisis, the banks for the most part exited the business, and the insurance companies came back and absorbed the bulk of the business at triple the wrap fees. After some uncertain years on wrap capacity, enough insurance companies have reentered the business that capacity concerns have disappeared.

WHY INVESTORS LIKE STABLE VALUE

Investors make stable value the top fixed income 401(k) asset classes, for three major reasons.
1. Higher returns than other stable assets like money market.
2. Less risk to principal than bond funds
3. Less correlation to stocks than either bonds or cash

Stable value funds outperform money market funds during most market environments. In fact, according to the Hueler Companies FirstSource Separate Account Stable Value Index, stable value funds have outperformed money market funds more than 85 percent of the time. An individual who invested in stable value funds in 1987 rather than money market funds received an additional 15 percent cumulative return or approximately one percent more returns per year, year after year.[12]

Morningstar Direct reports the typical stable-value fund yielded around 2% in 2013 and 2014, and it has yielded about 1% for the year to date 2015 which is still far above the Morningstar Taxable Money Market Index, which has yielded close to zero during the same time periods.[13]

Stable value funds provide higher returns because they hold intermediate-maturity bonds plus companion wrapper agreements providing protection of principal and accumulated earnings for investors. As a result, stable value funds tend to produce returns over the long-term roughly similar to intermediate-maturity bond funds. Unlike bond funds, however, stable value funds do not fluctuate in principal with changes in interest rates, so their volatility or risk is substantially less than bond funds.[14]

Because stable value has less correlation to stocks than other conservative investments, it is a more effective tool to modulate risk and return in an investor's retirement portfolio than money market or bond funds.[15]

CHAPTER ONE
DEFINING STABLE VALUE

Stable value has existed since the advent of U.S. tax-qualified defined contribution plans in the 1970s. All stable-value funds use guaranteed investment contracts (GICs) to provide them book-value accounting, which allows for a smoothing of returns and no negative periods. Traditional GICs are similar to certificates of deposit purchased at banks having a stated rate and maturity, but are sold by insurance companies. While bond funds can have negative returns for a quarter, stable value funds cannot.

There are three basic categories of stable value or GIC's: (1) The original *general account* or *traditional GIC*, (2) the *insurance company separate account GIC* and (3) the *synthetic GIC*, sometimes known as a *wrap*.

The U.S. pension trade press on stable-value funds focuses primarily on the synthetic GIC wrap-type products dominating the mega-plan market in the last ten years.

Stable value is a unique asset class available primarily in US based defined contribution plans, best known as the 401(k) market. Stable value seeks to offer capital preservation, liquidity, with returns typically higher than other similar options such as money market funds. Stable value investment options may be offered by investment managers, trust companies, or insurance companies in various structures.

the use of stable value investment contracts, issued by banks, insurance companies, and other financial institutions, convey to the investment option the ability to carry certain assets at book value, maintain principal value and minimize return volatility.

STABLE VALUE PRODUCT ALTERNATIVES

There are two other primary stable value product types, generically known as "traditional guaranteed investment contracts" and the hybrid "insurance company separate account" which looks on the surface more like a synthetic, but in ownership and risk is much closer to a traditional GIC.

Traditional GICs, which are issued solely by insurance companies, are the more straightforward of the two. The issuing insurance company simply guarantees the invested principal amount and pays a specified rate of return (which may adjust periodically) for a certain period of time. The issuer buys assets matched to the liability and the underlying assets are owned and managed by the issuer. Thus, with traditional GICs, the contractual guarantees are based solely on the issuer's claims-paying ability.

Guaranteed Investment Contract (GIC)

A stable value investment contracts (typically a group annuity contract) issued by an insurance company that pays a specified rate of return for a specific period of time, offers book value accounting, typically pays benefits to plan participants, and provides annuities upon request. These contracts are also known as guaranteed insurance contracts or guaranteed interest contracts and may be backed by either an issuer's general account assets or separate account assets. In all cases, the insurance company owns the invested assets and the obligation to the contract-holder is backed by the full financial strength and credit of the issuer. A GIC that is held as an investment by a stable value investment option is typically known as a traditional GIC, while a GIC offered as the sole stable value investment option is more generally known as a guaranteed insurance account.

Synthetic GICs, as the name implies, are structured differently, but deliver the same essential stable value benefits. It starts with an underlying portfolio of fixed-income securities owned by the plan, but with the overlay of the synthetic GIC structure, provided by a contract issued by an insurance company or bank it provides the smooth no loss features of other traditional stable value. Synthetic GICs are sometimes called "wrappers" or "wrap contracts" because they "wrap" a specific portfolio with contractual benefits.

Generally, though the specific contract form and terms may differ depending on the issuer, the wrapper provides for principal protection and a stable rate of return based on the return of the underlying assets. To stabilize the return, the wrap issuer uses a crediting rate formula to amortize the portfolio's gains and losses over time, while ensuring total return performance is ultimately passed through to participants. The crediting rate is guaranteed to be positive at all times, regardless of the performance of the underlying assets — the exception being that defaulted or impaired securities are technically excluded from wrap coverage. In practice the exception through a device called a credit bucket absorbs defaults in a diversified bond portfolio up to 5% of total assets.

> **Synthetic GIC (also known as a "synthetic" or "synthetic investment contract")**
> A stable value investment structure that offers similar characteristics as a guaranteed investment contract, i.e., pays a specified rate of return for a specific period of time, is benefit-responsive, and offers book value accounting. A synthetic GIC includes an asset ownership component and a contractual component that is intended to be valued at book value. The associated assets backing the contract's book value are owned and held in the name of the plan or the plan's trustee. Such associated assets typically consist of a diversified fixed income portfolio, including but not limited to treasury, government, mortgage, and/or corporate securities of high average credit quality. To support the book value obligation, the contract-holder relies first on any associated assets and then, to the extent those assets are insufficient, the financial backing of the wrap issuer. Wrap contracts can be issued by banks, insurance companies, or other financial institutions.

Today, most 401(k) stable value funds are a bond portfolio wrapped in synthetic GICs, or an insurance company separate account or general account product. In aggregate, 401(k) funds now consist of around seventy-five percent of the dollars in synthetic GICs and twenty-five percent other GIC's.[16]

Stable Value delivers bond-like returns while maintaining low volatility. The returns come from the underlying bonds which deliver higher returns through duration and credit spread. Stable value funds historically have maintained duration of two to four years, so they are able to capture returns at the intermediate range of the yield curve. In contrast, money market funds typically have a duration of far less than one year, so they are able to capture returns at the short end of the yield curve.

Stable value funds invest longer than cash, and therefore capture the expected uptick in yields, but they also have to keep volatility low and still offer participants book value liquidity at any time. The mechanics of stable value create smoothing effect which is achieved by a crediting rate formula amortizing the portfolio's gains and losses over time. Synthetic based stable value fund are evergreen in nature, i.e. they have no pre-defined maturity date, which allows the duration of the portfolio (unless it is changed for portfolio or risk management purposes) to remain fairly constant.

A constant duration, in turn, allows the stable value provider to continually amortize the portfolio's gains and losses. In effect, fund participants are continuously shielded from the short-term volatility associated with a two-to-four-year duration portfolio. This does not mean stable value is without risks for either participants or providers. Stable value providers, such as insurance companies and banks, mitigate their risk largely by being good at predicting and underwriting participant behavior. Underwriters for the providers looking at long term data know people tend to use less liquidity than they think they need in a 401(k) type plan. They know the vast majority of participants, because of tax penalties and simple investor inertia, tend to leave their money in stable value options for a fairly long time. Providers are willing, therefore, to guarantee a fixed rate for a traditional GIC or a minimum zero percent crediting rate each quarter for a synthetic GIC, because they are fairly certain there will not be a run on the bank.

It is important to note, although stable value contracts are as liquid as any other 401(k) option at the individual participant level; they have significant liquidity restrictions at the plan level under certain circumstances. In practice, however, most DC plans do not need the additional liquidity, so many find the incremental liquidity risk more than compensated for by stable values positive return characteristics.

Aside from liquidity risk, plan sponsors also pay great attention to the dimension of credit risk in stable value. This is especially important for the stable value options consisting of only one insurance company general account GIC (or insurance company separate account GIC) structure. Therefore these structures are exposed to single entity credit risk of the insurance company. As mentioned earlier, credit risk played an important role in the evolution of stable value product alternatives from general account GICs to separate account GICs and eventually to synthetic GICs, which greatly diminish credit risk. Credit risk can be managed in a number of ways including using general account GIC's from multiple issuers and diversifying within the synthetic structure.

> **Credit Risk**
>
> **The risk that an investment will default, i.e., the borrower or guarantor (the bond or investment contract issuer) will not pay principal and interest as scheduled. (See also impaired securities.)**

For stable value portfolios using synthetic GICs, credit risk is low since the plan retains asset ownership and the wrap contract covers the difference between market value and book value, i.e., the wrap provider must pay only if total book value withdrawals exceed the market value of the portfolio's underlying securities. Typically, market-to-book value shortfalls range from only one to five percent. Because of this, it has been demonstrated the default risk of synthetic GICs is less than one-tenth of a traditional GIC issued by the same company.[17] Many stable value managers, however, still opt to diversify with two or more wrappers and may limit the credit quality of the wrapper to a minimum of A or AA. The main reason to diversify has been a number of wrappers have left the business because of low profits. What typically happens when a wrapper leaves the business (or, in an extreme case, fails) is the other wrappers in the plan will agree to take on their share of the wrap.

Through the wrap contract, the fund is insured by a third party. The wrap contract sets a guaranteed interest rate. If the rate of return drops below the guaranteed rate, the insurer pays the difference. If the rate of return is higher than the set return, the fund pays the insurer the difference.

The largest mega plans: the Fortune 50 and most Fortune 500 firms have synthetic stable value in their 401(k) plans. With synthetic GICs, the 401(k) plan owns the underlying bonds comprising typically 95% to 100% of the total value. While short-term performance issues are possible, the synthetic GIC or wrap structure is considered by most experts as the best structure a plan can be in.

With the other two categories—insurance company separate account and general account GICs—the plan does not own any securities but solely owns a contract with an insurance company. The Mega plans fearful of potential litigation under the Employee Retirement Income Security Act (ERISA) plans abandoned general account GICs over 20 years ago after defaults by Executive Life and Confederation Life in 1992. Mega ERISA plans for the most part abandoned insurance company separate account stable value a decade ago because of concerns that even the reduced single-entity credit risk could be a fiduciary liability. However single entity general account and separate account product is still prevalent in many plans over $100 million in size, and is in the majority of plans under $100 million.

As a group, DC plan participants tend to be a conservative lot. Writing in the *Financial Analysts Journal*, Saraoglu and Detzler highlight the unique preferences and constraints of individual investors and specifically cite "preservation of principal" as a major factor in fund selection.[18] No losses is one reason stable value funds have been extremely popular with participants. But stable value also adds "juice" in the form of consistently higher returns than principal-safe money market funds. In fact, stable value offers total returns similar to those of intermediate bonds with little of the volatility associated with bonds, as illustrated below:

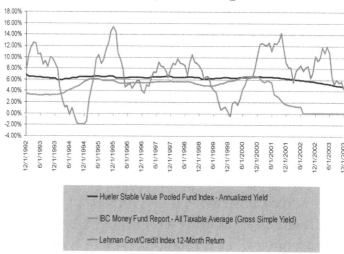

Historical yield comparisons

— Hueler Stable Value Pooled Fund Index - Annualized Yield
— IBC Money Fund Report - All Taxable Average (Gross Simple Yield)
— Lehman Gov't/Credit Index 12-Month Return

While the chart above offers dramatic historical evidence of stable value's benefits from a broad market perspective, it's important to note that such experience is validated in the real world of individual fund management. Since 1983, Paul Lipson has managed the $3.2 billion stable value fund of the Federal Reserve Employee Benefits System — a fund extremely popular with the plan's 33,000 participants, drawing an overall allocation of more than 68 percent. According to Lipson, *"We've delivered a return equal to or greater than that of the Lehman Brothers Aggregate Bond Index over time at one-quarter of the risk."*[19]

Participants seem intuitively drawn to the potent combination of low cash-like volatility and higher bond-like returns. Yet, it is precisely this hybrid quality that historically vexed firms providing asset allocation advice to 401(k) plans and participants. For years, advice providers either left stable value out of asset allocation models or else lumped it with short- to intermediate-term bonds, without capturing the benefit of dampened volatility afforded by stable value's book value guarantee. Major asset allocation advice providers, such as Financial Engines, mPower, and Morningstar's Clear Future, have made minor inroads in upgrading their methodology. However, full credit for the bond-like returns, money market fund-like volatility, low correlation with equities, and generally lower expense ratios compared to bond funds has not been achieved.[20]

CHAPTER TWO
INSURANCE COMPANY GENERAL ACCOUNT

BLAST FROM THE PAST

This product can work well for clients if priced (to yield) competitively, but the lack of transparency makes this extremely difficult to gauge. The lack of transparency in general account stable value has allowed insurance companies in some instances to overcharge for this version of Stable Value. However, pricing varies greatly by insurance company, by size of the client, and in different points of time. Since general account spread is not scalable (like the investment management fees underlying synthetic stable value), it can be more attractive relatively for smaller 401(k) plans under $200 million in assets.

The 2008 financial crisis created a wrap shortage in the synthetic GIC market. Unlike the other GIC markets, the synthetic market has evolved so that over 2/3's of providers are not insurance companies but most of the largest global banks, all of which been affected severely by the crisis. Post crisis led to insurance companies trying to gain back market share for their separate account and general account products, which provide a higher profit for insurance companies but carry higher risks and higher fees for plans.   While this strategy continues to work with government plans outside of ERISA regulation, corporate plans for the most part would not go back to general account.

In recent years low rate environment, the ability of insurance companies to use higher risk investments such as private placements, real estate, high yield bonds, hedge funds, and equity and use leverage on their balance sheets, can give them a yield advantage over many other versions of stable value.   However this yield advantage comes at a much higher risk than a diversified synthetic product, and the spread is usually not high enough to compensate for the additional risks.

In 2008 Federal Reserve Chairman Ben Bernanke said *"workers whose 401(k) plans had purchased $40 billion of insurance from AIG against the risk that their stable-value funds would decline in value would have seen that insurance disappear."*[21]

Many investment professionals believe that a plan sponsor is taking a severe fiduciary risk by having a single contract with any one entity such as AIG. After 2008 and Dodd-Frank the government came up with a the concept of a systemically important financial institution (*SIFI*) to be a bank, insurance company, or other financial institution whose failure might trigger a financial crisis. These entities would have much higher capital reserve requirements and increased government scrutiny. So far the US Government has named 3 insurance companies Metlife, AIG, and Prudential as SIFI's or "too big to fail". [22] These 3 insurance companies who all issue General Account GIC's are not marketing themselves as safer, but are actively trying to get away from SIFI status with its higher capital requirements (leading to less profit).

While it could be argued a plan is taking less risk by assuming the single insurance company backing the stable value option is too big to fail and has an implied government guarantee, the lack of buy in by the insurance companies themselves make it too risky for a long term bet based on this pseudo government backing.

GENERAL ACCOUNT

The Stable Value Investment Association (SVIA) defines *general account* as "the primary part of a life insurance company's balance sheet containing the capital and surplus and reserves for guaranteed liabilities. Traditional GICs are backed by the issuer's General Account."[23]

The holder of a general account GIC is taking on the risk the individual insurance company could default on its obligation to repay principal and pay interest. However, the GIC holder has a slightly higher claim on the insurance company's reserves than a bondholder would have and a much higher claim than a stockholder.

The National Association of Government Defined Contribution Administrators, Inc. (NAGDCA) in September 2010 created a brochure with this characterization of general account stable value:

Due to the fact the plan sponsor does not own the underlying investments, the portfolio holdings, performance, risk, and management fees are generally not disclosed. This limits the ability of plan sponsors to compare returns with other SVFs [stable-value funds]. It also makes it nearly impossible for plan sponsors to know the fees (which can be increased without disclosure) paid by participants in these funds—a critical component of a fiduciary's responsibility. [24]

In May 2010, the *Wall Street Journal* reported:

Amid the shortage of wrap insurance, though, some firms are seizing an opportunity to reintroduce older types of stable-value products that are backed by a single insurer and carry considerable risks.
OneAmerica Financial Partners Inc.'s American United Life Insurance Co., for example, last month launched a stable-value product backed by its own general-account assets. In such products, investors are taking on the risk that this single issuer could go belly up. [25]

General account products, because of legal liability, are avoided by most of the larger corporate plans, but are still used in smaller plans and in corners of the DC market like 457 and 403(b) not governed by ERISA and thus subject to less liability.

SPREAD = FEES = LIABILITY

Insurance products differ from investment management products in that much of the profit comes from spread not fees. Insurance companies compare this to the spread a bank makes on CDs. Spread is a main profit generator for insurance companies and banks, where their investments make more than their cost of deposits or funds— To repeat from the NAGDCA brochure, *"It also makes it nearly impossible for plan sponsors to know the fees (which can be increased without disclosure) paid by participants in these funds—a critical component of a fiduciary's responsibility."*[26]

Spread is complicated to measure because you have to quantify what a plan should be compensated for taking on the single entity risk of the insurance company. A starting point to measure this is in the Credit Default Swap market, which is regularly priced over 200 basis points to insure the credit risk of many insurance companies.

DOL RULES

The 2012 Department of Labor rules on fee disclosure (408b-2) and fiduciary duty are still being evolving, it's likely three aspects of general account stable value products will continue to be problematic:

1. *High stable-value fees and spread subsidizing administrative costs.* revenue from general stable value options have typically subsidized administration costs, making some participants pay higher administration costs than those in mutual funds, and making products appear competitive in requests for proposal looking at per head administrative costs.
2. *Fees and commissions are to be fully disclosed.* Insurance companies are still fighting not to disclose any spread profits. These excessive profits, even if called *spread*, act like fees and are used like fees. Commission kickbacks to consultants with insurance licenses are common in plans with general and separate account stable value.
3. *Higher levels of fiduciary duty for vendors.* Since general stable-value assets are on the balance sheet of the insurance company, this creates an inherent conflict between the fiduciary care of pension investors and company shareholders.

An ERISA fiduciary with any single entity separate account or general account insurance stable-value product should ask five questions:

1. Is my insurance company "too big to fail"?
2. Which state regulates my contract? How solid is this regulation?

3. Do I want to own the underlying assets or a piece of paper from an insurance company during the next financial crisis?
4. Am I comfortable taking single-entity credit risk when better diversified options are available?
5. Is the insurance company accepting fiduciary liability?

I contend most ERISA plans should not take on the single-entity credit risk and liquidity risk of an insurance company, especially in the aftermath of AIG and in the so-called end of too big to fail.

Large ERISA plans abandoned these options after the 1992 Executive and Confederation Life defaults. However 403b plans and 457 plans, which are currently outside ERISA, have huge balances in General Account stable value. For many small plans this is the sole type of plan offered. Many times the exit provisions are so onerous they are referred to as "Roach Motels" via paraphrasing the advertising slogan "plan sponsors can check in but cannot check out".

PRUDENT USES FOR GENERAL ACCOUNT

The case can made for general account options in the smaller 401(k) plans under $200 million in assets typically offered by bundled insurance company providers. This is because in many structures and platforms for plans under $200 million synthetic based stable is not available.

For many years and up until recently the Federal Reserve and the University of California held diversified portfolios of general account GIC's. With typical allocations not exceeding 5% per issuer the single entity, credit risk was largely diversified away. The ladder approach insured structured maturities and ready liquidity. However, as the number of GIC issuers went under 20 it became difficult to build a diversified portfolio, as the industry moved away toward synthetics. Some stable value pooled funds still use diversified general account GICS including Vanguard, but they have become smaller parts of the portfolio as the number of issuers has shrank. One boutique firm FCM still works with GIC ladders and still promotes them as value added in a rising rate environment. [27]

Public DC plans or 457 plans are not subject to ERISA, so the insurance companies have tended to hold onto this business. However even this industry has a hard time justifying the single entity risk of general account and has put their marketing muscle behind Insurance Company Separate Account. The industry group NAGDCA turned against general account: *Due to the fact that the plan sponsor does not own the underlying investments, the portfolio holdings, performance, risk, and management fees are generally not disclosed. This limits the ability of plan sponsors to compare returns with other SVFs.* Large ERISA plans abandoned General account over 20 years ago after the Executive Life and Confederation Life defaults of 1992. Large Non-ERISA 457 and 403(b) have been much slower in getting out of these products. The new DOL rules in my opinion have started to reduce general account products in 401k's between the size of $200 million and $500 million to the disappointment of the insurance industry.[28]

General account market share continues to go down in 401(k), and in the larger 457 plans. General Account is holding strong in the 403(b) with most of it with quasi non-profit TIAA-CREF, and assisted by legal issues for synthetics. While you still see some general account product targeted to the under $200 million market, they will continue to be under fire.[29] The NAGDCA brochure I think fairly address general account and join's the industry consensus in distancing itself from single entity credit risk.

RECENT USES

General account products with their higher yielding balance sheet assets over traditional fixed income could potentially be good products for even larger plans. However insurance companies seem determined to make large fees off this product as evidenced by Prudential's report to stockholders on making 200 basis points on the product. [30] According to a report by the consulting firm Blue Prairie the average crediting rate as of December 2014 for their General Account GIC Average: 2.15% while there Private Synthetic GIC Average: 1.90% [31] This recent yield pickup of only 25 basis points is not enough in my opinion to justify the additional risks for plans with access to synthetic stable value.

CHAPTER THREE

INSURANCE COMPANY SEPARATE ACCOUNT: SMOKE AND MIRRORS

Stable value in an insurance company separate account was pushed hard after the 1992 defaults as an improvement on general account for larger plans. However, by the year 2000, most of the largest plans had moved on to synthetics, because the same overall risk and transparency issues in general account still carry over to insurance company separate account. During the 2008 Synthetic GIC shortage, many insurance companies tried to reenter the market by selling separate account stable value as being similar to a synthetic wrapped stable value fund.

With Insurance company separate account, as in general account, the plan does not own the funds underlying bonds. In a separate account product; the plans assets are still on the balance sheet of the insurance company. A separate account gives the *appearance* the plan has a unique portfolio, but in the end, all the plan has is a piece of paper—a claim on the assets of the insurance company. This insurance guarantee can also widely vary based on the state of issuance.

According to a 2014 study by the Chicago based consulting firm Blue Prairie: Separate Account stable value had on average a duration 60% higher than diversified synthetic based stable value (4.42 vs. 2.53). Separate account products had much lower overall credit ratings, and invested in high yield and non-rated assets not allowed in synthetics. This additional risk and duration did lead to higher crediting rates of 3.03% for Separate Account over 1.90% for larger Synthetic portfolios.[32] Insurance companies in separate accounts invest more like they do in general account as both are on the insurance company balance sheet. Separate accounts many times do not have to follow client specific investment guidelines and can use leverage.

The AICPA, in 2009 testimony to the DOL, states plans cannot solely rely on their Stable Value managers or providers, they must understand their underlying SV contracts themselves or look to independent 3rd parties. [33] This view is reinforced by the new DOL 408(b) (2) disclosure rules. A survey in July 2010 shows after FinReg and the new DOL rules, 46% of plans said they need increased scrutiny around Stable Value Plans. [34] The new disclosure rules will most likely lead to a decreasing use of Insurance Company Separate account in ERISA plans.

PUBLIC PLAN USE OF INSURANCE COMPANY SEPARATE ACCOUNT

Public DC plans also known as 457 plans are not subject to ERISA, including its new transparency and fee disclosure rules. Insurance companies have continued to thrive with separate account business in this non-regulated market. The Public DC Trade group is the National Association of Government Defined Contribution Administrators (NAGDCA). NAGDCA has shown concern for the single entity risk of general account but still seems supportive of Insurance Company Separate Account.

The largest (1000+) ERISA plans for the most part abandoned Separate Account stable value a decade ago. However of the larger Public 457 plans only the 30 or so largest and most sophisticated have gone to synthetics. This still leaves many large over $500 million public plans in insurance company separate account.

Many in the Public 457 market evidenced by the NAGDCA publication make a strong distinction between General Account and Separate account. I see this as a surface distinction as the underlying structures however are very similar in risk and fees.
I would apply the same applications to fees to Insurance Company Separate account that the NAGDCA brochure applies to general account. "It *also makes it nearly impossible for plan sponsors to know the fees (which can be increased without disclosure) paid by participants in these funds – a critical component of a fiduciary's responsibility.*[35]"

In my 7 years experience as an insurance officer pricing all 3 versions of stable value, we classified both separate and general account stable value as spread product, while synthetics GIC's were different and considered a fee product. As discussed earlier general account spread product nets companies close to 200 basis points, my estimate is Separate Account product nets between 125 and 175 basis points, based on discussions I have had over the years on pricing.

While insurance company separate accounts can have the appearance of a synthetic, in a crisis they will act much more like their general account cousins. And while the spread made on them is less than general account and estimated at 175 basis points, it is still far more profitable than synthetics at 20 basis points, even if you add another 30 basis points for active bond management they may have to pay to an outside bond manager.

At the 2004 NAGDCA conference, a panel of consultants estimated insurance company bundled providers make 70% of their total plan profit off of the stable value option, by issuing their own separate account GICs. Talk also revolved around this huge Stable Value profit, allowing these bundled providers to subsidize administrative costs and make them appear to be low bidders and win business on Public RFP's versus more unbundled approaches.

The new DOL rules strictly forbid this practice of cost shifting in 401(k) plans. Hopefully the new DOL rule will push 457 plans to examine the practice of the participants holding stable value subsidizing the administrative fees for the participants who do not or hold small amounts of stable value. This 125 to 175 basis points spread in a separate account structure enables insurance companies not only to subsidize administration fees but gives them the ability to give undisclosed compensation to consultants who hold insurance licenses. Public plans should hire truly independent consultants who do not hold a brokerage or insurance license to make the best stable value selection.

I disagree strongly with some of the language on Insurance Company Separate Accounts in the NAGDCA brochure. While technically correct in admitting the insurer still owns and controls the assets, I find the following language confusing *"However due to the fact the assets are segregated, the plan sponsor may have additional transparency regarding portfolio holdings, performance and fees.* [36]
The critical word is "may" at the insurance companies' discretion. Again they may not, or give some transparency some time, but when times are bad shut it off. If you want to test this ask them to put in writing that you have full transparency on holdings, performance and fees. The word "may" in the small print of your stable value contract is critical to understanding your real risk.

The brochure makes the following statement *"identifies a segregated pool of assets held and owned by an insurance company but distinct from the insurer's general investment account, and therefore, not subject to claims of creditors should the insurance company become insolvent."* This statement is misleading at best.

Managing an Insurance Company Separate Account product I became well versed on solvency issues when trying to sell the product. I reviewed detailed legal opinions on what would happen in a default situation. In the event of default, Separate Accounts would be above General account, but would be classified as a Class 2 priority. Class One would be payroll etc. of employees, while general account would be in the 3rd or 4th tier. Within class 2 the separate account would rank equal or pari passu with the claims of life insurance policyholders.

However a bankruptcy judge could control the order in the Class 2 to put all of the policy holders ahead of the separate account holders. In a bankruptcy situation while you are ahead in line of General account products, it could still be months or years before you could get your money out of a separate account.

Going beyond the scope of the brochure, I have created a test for this product to see how segregated it is. Ask the insurance company to put it in writing if they defaulted or were even downgraded, they would wire "your" securities to you within 5 days, or 5 weeks or 5 months. I contend they will not because the entire concept of a separate account as segregated and available like bonds held at your custodian is, in my opinion, a ruse.

While separate accounts can vary greatly according to the state in which they're issued—from a industry friendly regulatory state like Iowa to the most heavily regulated state, New York—the basic problem of being an account on the insurance company balance sheet remains.

The NAGDCA brochure makes another troubling assertion *"In a pooled structure, the underlying investment strategy and inherent risks associated with Separate Account SVFs are similar to those found in "synthetic GIC structures."* This is misleading and overall not true. You still have the much higher single entity credit risk as most synthetic pools have 6 wrappers or more. Again the collective investment trust would own only a contract with a Separate account, but own the underlying securities with the synthetic. The internalized fees on a credit risk adjusted basis would be much higher as well for the separate account in most cases.

INSURANCE COMPANY SEPARATE ACCOUNT HISTORY

With this option the plan still holds a contract with the insurance company (not bonds) but they do have a segregated account on the insurance companies balance sheet with many times specific bonds tied to the plan sponsors specific account. Some even allow you to pick another outside manager from a lineup but still on the Insurance company books. While it is superior to general account you are still taking single entity credit risk but are higher up in line in a bankruptcy. You still have, for example, many times eight-year exits giving it the same "Roach Motel" features you see in general account stable value products.

As an example, in the 1992 Executive Life and Confederation Life defaulted and the separate account holders eventually received 100% of principal, however this 100% payout is not guaranteed. It could be conceivable a judge could "cram down" this amount to 50 cents or 75 cents on the dollar. A 2009 Barron's story on a Separate Account structure by the City of San Francisco outlines a combination of issues with these strategies. [37]

Separate accounts were created in the 1960's to allow pensions to diversify into equities, which have evolved into the variable annuity markets of today. Insurance companies typically are not subject to Federal Bankruptcy laws but to state laws in insolvency. Most states have adopted some type of insulation of separate accounts which put them at a higher level in the credit hierarchy than a general account holder. Most states have adopted the NAIC Model Law for separate accounts and there are 5 different state AG opinions on the solvency of separate accounts. [38]

S&P, in its ratings, say states differ so much in their credit protection for Separate Accounts, identical contracts could results in different ratings in different states. [39]

"While there have been insolvencies involving separate accounts, the circumstances under which a separate account might be consolidated with the insurer's general account remain substantially undefined. Furthermore, it is not clear in most states whether separate account performance guarantees from an insolvent issuer would rank as policyholder obligations. Additional uncertainty is created because, in some states, the status of GIC's as insurance policies has not been settled. [40]

While the Department of Labor rules on disclosure (408b-2) and fiduciary duty are still not crystal clear it's likely three aspects of insurance company separate account stable value products will continue to be problematic:

1. *High stable-value fees and spread subsidizing administrative costs.* Revenue from separate account stable value options have typically subsidized administration costs, making some participants pay higher administration costs than those in mutual funds, and making products appear competitive in requests for proposal looking at per head administrative costs.
2. *Fees and commissions are to be fully disclosed.* Insurance companies are still fighting not to disclose any spread profits. These excessive profits, even if called *spread*, act like fees and are used like fees. Undisclosed commission to consultants with insurance licenses are common in plans with general and separate account stable value.
3 *Higher levels of fiduciary duty for vendors.* Since separate account stable-value assets are on the balance sheet of the insurance company, this creates an inherent conflict between the fiduciary care of pension investors and company shareholders.

An ERISA fiduciary or public plan fiduciary with any single entity separate account insurance stable-value product needs to ask five questions:

- Is my insurance company "too big to fail"?
- Which state regulates my contract? How solid is this regulation?

- Do I want to own the underlying assets or a piece of paper from an insurance company during the next financial crisis?
- Am I comfortable taking single-entity credit risk when better diversified options are available?
- Is the insurance company accepting fiduciary liability?

An ERISA fiduciary or public plan fiduciary with any single entity separate account insurance stable-value product needs to ask five questions:

1. Is my insurance company "too big to fail"?
2. Which state regulates my contract? How solid is this regulation?
3. Do I want to own the underlying assets or a piece of paper from an insurance company during the next financial crisis?
4. Am I comfortable taking single-entity credit risk when better diversified options are available?
5. Is the insurance company accepting fiduciary liability?

CONCLUSION

Stable value in an Insurance Company Separate Account is many times sold as similar to a synthetic wrapped stable value, but in my opinion, it is not. You do not own the underlying bonds, they are still on the balance sheet of the insurance company. It may appear you have a unique portfolio, but it is mostly smoke and mirrors. All you have in the end is a piece of paper, a claim on the assets of the insurance company. When I was a separate account product manager I would have clients ask about the performance of their portfolio. I asked our investment guys and they laughed, because they managed all the assets (separate account and general account) in the one large pool, and there was an accounting guy on another floor creating the separate accounts for show, marking securities like you would for collateral. While there are some separate accounts managed by firms outside the insurance company in which you can more readily identify assets and performance, you really need to examine the details of the arrangement. Regardless, even the outside independent bond manager still legally works for the insurance company and the assets belong to the company not the plan.

How many large government plans continue to take the single entity credit risk and liquidity risk of an Insurance Company separate account still puzzles me in the aftermath of AIG and in the so called end of "too big to fail". Most people remember that pre 2008 crash AIG was rated AAA and was considered extremely safe.

How do you know your insurance company behind your separate account is not the next AIG? Given the high hidden spread enabling insurance companies to manipulate administrative pricing and even some consultants, separate accounts should be troubling to larger plans.

In the instance especially for plans under $200 million synthetic stable value options may not be available, and the choice may between an insurance company separate account and money market. In those cases a stronger case can be made, but it all comes down to the specifics of the option.

CHAPTER FOUR

SYNTHETIC GIC'S OR WRAPS

Generally, the larger plans in the industry have transitioned to synthetic stable value structures. This not only includes the Fortune 500 corporate 401(k) plans, but also the large collective investments trusts run by the large bundled 401(k) providers. Leading synthetic managers include: Galliard ($49 billion), BNY Mellon ($14 billon), Invesco, ($30 billion) and Goldman ($30 billion) of assets of the largest corporate plans. The large stable value collective trust managers include Wells Fargo ($28 billion) 2 by Fidelity ($24 billion), Vanguard ($17 billion), T. Rowe ($11 billion) and others and are covered in detail in the next chapter. [41]

Synthetic GICs are sometimes called "wrappers" or "wrap contracts" because they "wrap" a specific portfolio with contractual benefits. To stabilize the return, the wrap issuer uses a crediting rate formula to amortize the portfolio's gains and losses over time, while ensuring total return performance (net of fees) is ultimately passed through to participants.[42]

As indicated by the Hewitt survey: When the best synthetic diversified stable value options are provided they are the dominant fixed income option chosen by participants. Synthetic options have their own issues to a lesser degree. Instead of a 100% loss with a financial entity default, their loss could be from 2% to 20% depending on the underlying portfolios. Many by using 3 or 4 wrappers diversify this risk. The range from 2% to 20% is dependent on the underlying investment performance.

Legally the main differentiator of a Synthetic GIC is the plan or stable value pooled fund retains full ownership of the supporting fixed income assets. [43] The synthetic GIC can take many forms if issued by insurance company it can be a group annuity or a funding agreement.
If issued by a bank or other financial company it can be structured as a swap agreement, investment management agreement, or even a general contract without the regulatory language known as a book value agreement or benefit responsive contract. [44] From a risk perspective with value at risk the credit exposure the plan has to the insurer is one tenth or less. [45]

CREDITING RATE AND CONTRACT TERMS

"How does the crediting rate work in a Synthetic GIC?" is an important question to answer. Crediting rates applied to the portfolio are determined as a function of the underlying yield of the bonds being wrapped, as well as the prevailing yields available at the inception of the fund. For example, a fund started in 2005 might have a crediting rate near five percent, while a fund wrapped in 2015's lower rate environment would yield under two percent. One variable determines how much participants ultimately earn in a synthetic GIC — the performance of the underlying bond portfolio. [46] Yet the crediting rate is also a stabilizing mechanism for the synthetic, amortizing the portfolio's gains and losses over time so participants are shielded from dramatic short-term swings. To achieve this stabilization crediting rate methodologies also factor in portfolio duration and the market to book value ratio.

Below is an example of how a crediting rate formula works under different interest rate scenarios with different portfolios. Most formulas are employed on an

Scenario 3: 4% yield	
5 yr duration	Crediting Rate:
Mkt/Book 102	4.43%
Mkt/Book 100	4.00%
Mkt/Book 98	3.63%

Scenario 4: 6% yield	
5 yr duration	Crediting Rate:
Mkt/Book 102	6.38%
Mkt/Book 100	6.00%
Mkt/Book 98	5.58%

overall portfolio and reset the crediting rate quarterly to reflect the underlying investment performance. (There have been cases where individual securities are wrapped and the crediting rate resets only with significant changes in cash flows; however, this use is declining.) The portfolio yield is the leading factor in setting the crediting rate, but given a certain yield, the next biggest factors are the market to book value ratio of the portfolio, and the underlying duration.

A deduction of ten basis points for a typical wrap fee is also reflected in the table below:

Scenario 1: 4% yield	
3 yr duration	Crediting Rate:
Mkt/Book 102	4.69%
Mkt/Book 100	4.00%
Mkt/Book 98	3.36%

Scenario 2: 6% yield	
3 yr duration	Crediting Rate:
Mkt/Book 102	6.64%
Mkt/Book 100	6.00%
Mkt/Book 98	5.31%

Crediting rate formula = $i + [(MV - BV) / (MV \times D)]$ where:

i = portfolio yield
MV = portfolio market value
BV = portfolio book value
D = portfolio duration

It's important to note these scenarios should not be viewed comparatively (since a comparative examination would erroneously suggest a longer duration implies lower return volatility). Rather, they are intended to show in general terms, the interplay of factors in each discrete crediting rate calculation.

Since the crediting rate also acts as a smoothing mechanism, the portfolio duration affects the amount of time available to amortize gains or losses, and therefore the longer the duration the smaller the effect of underlying gains and losses on the crediting rate. The market/book value ratio affects the crediting rate in a similar way. A positive market/book ratio of 102, for example (which is common in a falling rate environment), will boost the crediting rate over the underlying yield. Conversely, a negative market/book ratio of 98 will result in a lower crediting rate versus the underlying yield.

The specific crediting rate formula used above is called the market value duration formula: *(i + [(MV - BV) / (MV x D)])*. Another formula used is a geometric version called compound amortization: *[(1+i)x(MV / BV)^(1/D)] − 1)*. A third formula called book value duration can also be used: *(i + [(MV - BV) / (BV x D)])*. The differences in the resulting crediting rates are extremely small —two to four basis points — and in the long run are not significant. Differences in crediting rates can also result from how different managers calculate duration. Some managers may actually use the duration of a benchmark portfolio in the crediting rate formula rather than the actual duration of the underlying securities. The yield (i) used in the formulas is predominately a duration market weighted bond equivalent yield, but some variations have occurred.

Types of wrap contracts vary by issuer. Insurance companies typically issue synthetics as group annuity contracts, while banks may issue wrap as "benefit responsive agreements," "repurchase agreements," or even swaps. But regardless of the issuer or contract type, all wrap contracts guarantee payments for participant withdrawals at book value. Accordingly, author Paul Donahue has argued a wrap is, by definition, an insurance contract not a derivative.[47] This is an important distinction because, pursuant to SOP 94-4, insurance contracts allow stable value book value accounting treatment, while derivatives are subject to more rigid mark to market accounting.[48] While the credit exposure is minimal, insurance company wraps could be viewed as higher in the claims priority hierarchy of the insurance company as compared to a contract issued by a bank where it may be more in line with senior debt or derivative-type contracts; however, most plans use bank and insurance contracts interchangeably.

Because all wrap contracts perform essentially the same function for a stable value fund, the particular form a given contract takes is not nearly as important a consideration for plan sponsors as the specific terms and obligations under the contract.[49]

One of the most important considerations when it comes to contract terms and obligations is whether the contract is "participating," "non-participating," or a combination of the two known as a "hybrid" contract. Participating versus non-participating refers to the degree to which the wrap issuer insures the stable value fund and its participants against negative investment and cash flow experience.

In a non-participating contract, the fund participants *do not* participate in the fund's investment or cash flow risk, i.e., the wrap issuer fully insures the fund against negative experience. In a participating contract, the fund participants *do* participate in the fund's investment or cash flow experience, i.e., the issuer transfers this risk back to the fund via the crediting rate formula. It is important to note the riskiest scenario is when rates rapidly rise (an inverted yield curve) and participants leave the plan or switch out of the stable value option. In this scenario, a participating contract's crediting rate would be adjusted to reflect market losses, and the wrapper pays a claim only if there is a book to market deficit after all participants have left the plan. Under a non-participating contract in this scenario, the risk to the wrap issuer would be unacceptably high. In addition, non-participating contracts offer fund participants no appreciable economic benefits under most interest rate scenarios. For these reasons, straight non-participating wrap contracts have disappeared.

Pre-2008 a few stable value managers still used some non-participating insurance protection to stabilize crediting rates for participants in rising rate environments. Some accomplished this with 25/75 or 30/70 participating/non-participating hybrid structures. Others used some type of "advance" contracts having non-participating-like effects on crediting rates. In these arrangements, the wrap issuer "advances" benefit payments from its general account and is repaid through the fund's cash flows, leaving the crediting rate unaffected.

Even Pre-2008, 100 percent participating contracts were the norm because they allowed much more flexibility in the underlying investments and are less expensive. The return picked up by using both longer duration and lower quality bonds offsets the additional stability in rising rate environments afforded by hybrid contracts.[50] Most managers and plans by 2005 that their investment structure gives them adequate liquidity and protection and have decided that the incremental protection of non-participating wraps is not justified by their higher costs.[51]

WRAPS GOING FORWARD

In and after the 2008 financial crisis there was a temporary wrap shortage. Also during this transition wraps became 100% participating, with tougher investment guidelines and higher fees. Wrap Capacity slowly started back in 2010 but was quickly coming back by 2012. The latest data came from an SVIA survey conducted in March 2015. The industry had $77.5 billion in potential new capacity in 2012, $103.5 billion in 2013, $87.8 billion in 2014, and another $79 billion for 2015.[52]

CHAPTER FIVE

POOLED FUNDS OR COLLECTIVE INVESTMENT TRUSTS

For a 401(k) plan or other DC plan with between $100 million and $500 million in assets, the collective investment trust (CIT) is probably the best way to access synthetic stable value with reasonable fees.

GROWTH OF POOLED FUNDS OR COLLECTIVE INVESTMENT TRUSTS

The Wall Street journal recently reported there are now more than 1,200 collective trusts, with at least $1.6 trillion in total assets in all asset classes including equity. At least $800 billion of CIT assets are held in defined-contribution plans, up from roughly $730 billion in 2009. [53]

The advantages of CIT's are most evident in lower fees. For example, one large stock manager managing funds for 401(k) plan sponsors charges 0.89% for a mutual fund and as little as 0.30% for assets greater than $140 million in a collective trust. *"Collective trusts provide the overall benefits of a mutual fund—such as professional investment management, a broadly diversified portfolio of holdings, and the like—generally at a much more effective price point,"* says Winfield Evens, a partner Aon Hewitt. [54] According to Hewitt Associates, the median expense ratio of some collective funds can be as much as 35 basis points lower than a similar styled mutual fund. [55]

"Low cost vehicles such as collective funds can help sponsors be better fiduciaries," added Greg Allen, President and Director of research at Callan Associates *"The fact that collective funds can only be held in qualified plans significantly reduces the possibility of trading abuses in these vehicles.... The fact that hedge funds cannot buy and sell collective funds provides a natural level of protection that can allow for less restrictive trading rules than are necessary in a mutual fund vehicle."* [56]

For Stable value CIT's in 1997 a small $1 million plan paid between 25 and 80 basis points with an average of 42 bps (not including wrap fees), also in 1997 a $10 million plan paid between 19 and 55 basis points with an average of 34. [57] Vanguard as of 12/31/14 listed total fees as 0.53% or 53 basis points but this also includes a 0.22% fee ($2.20 per $1,000 invested) paid to the issuers of synthetic investment contracts.[58] These CIT fees using synthetic based stable value are generally 50 to 75% less than either general account or separate account products.

STABLE VALUE IN CIT'S

Stable Value mutual funds were discontinued in 2004, so collective investment trusts are the only non-insurance (general account and separate account) vehicle for mid-size to smaller plans for stable value.

The history of stable value collective funds date back to 1981 and started with 70% of the plans sponsored by banks and the other 30% sponsored by the 401(k) providers loosely known as mutual fund companies. By 1997 these mutual fund companies held 70% of Stable Value Collective Assets led by Fidelity, Vanguard, T.Rowe, and 30% where held by banks. [59] In 2014, large stable value collective trusts continued to be dominated by the mutual fund companies with Fidelity ($24 billion), Vanguard ($17 billion) and T.Rowe ($11 billion), with one big bank exception Wells Fargo ($28 billion). [60]

For two decades, stable value has been a major force in the collective fund universe and its opportunities for future growth are rising in tandem with the growth of collective funds. As more plans come to realize the advantages of collective funds versus mutual funds in target-date, lifecycle and balanced options, stable value has the opportunity to capture market share from mutual fund options.

12 MONTH PUTS

Collective vehicles mix different plans so rules were set up to protect the fund as a whole. The synthetic stable value contracts while allowing plan participants total liquidity, need to restrict or control entire plans leaving at book value when the market value of the assets are below the book value. [61]
For large plans with individually managed synthetic contracts, exiting the entire plan can be accomplished in a time period equal to the duration of the underlying bonds, usually 2 to 4 years. But since any one plan in a collective vehicle is a smaller percentage, the industry practice has been more lenient with a maximum of 1 year or 12 months. If the market to book value is positive or near 100, plans can be let out sooner at book. Plans can also get out at market value sooner.

Many competitors of these CIT's try to make the 12 month put sound like a risky restriction when in fact it lowers the risks for the remaining participants. In 2012 this misperception was further fueled by one troubled bank collective fund removing its formal 12 month put and trying to spin it as a positive for participants, when in fact it decreased the liquidity greatly. Another fund with investment issues went from a 12 month to a 24 month put. These incidents however were outliers and the vast majority of Stable Value CIT's have operated 12 month puts for plans with no problems in recent years.

Hueler List of Participating Funds[62]

Fund Name
BMO Employee Benefit Stable Principal
Columbia Trust Stable Income Fund
Columbia Trust Stable Government Fund
Federated Capital Preservation Fund
FFTW Income Plus Fund
Galliard Managed Income Fund
ICMA-RC Vantage Trust PLUS Fund
INVESCO Stable Value Trust
John Hancock Stable Value Fund
JPMorgan Stable Asset Income Fund
Morley Stable Value Fund
Putnam Stable Value Fund
T. Rowe Price Stable Value Fund
Vanguard Retirement Savings Trust
Wells Fargo Stable Return Fund

This list of 15 is representative but does not include the 2 large Fidelity Stable Value Funds (known as MIPS and MIPS II), a number of private label bank funds and dozens of insurance company separate and general account funds. 14 of the 15 of the plans on this list are primarily synthetic GIC based with John Hancock being the exception.

However, many 401(k) plans under $200 million do not offer stable value because it is more efficient for their structure to contain solely mutual funds. While large pooled fund providers like Fidelity, Vanguard and T.Rowe price have stable value collective trusts they chose not to offer any stable value options to many plans under $200 million in assets. The administrative costs of mixing a CIT with mutual funds are given as the reason.

Three synthetic based stable value mutual funds were successful for investors up until 2004 when the SEC (My opinion because of political pressure from money market funds) shut them down for no rational reason. Thus the SEC has limited the access to the most efficient low risk low fee version of stable value to plans under $200 million.

CHAPTER SIX

CONSULTANT AND PLAN SPONSOR PERSPECTIVE

Since 2008 and the subsequent wrapper shortage there has been some frustration among large plan sponsors and their consultants with the complexity of stable value. However, with money market yields near zero, and issues with major bond managers there seem to be no real replacements for stable value.

CONSULTANT PERSPECTIVES

Angelo Auriemma director of investment advisory services for Plan Sponsor Advisors LLC, told participants at the Stable Value Investment Association's (SVIA) 2012 Annual Forum: "Then the financial crisis hit, and their questions, and concerns, started to change."[63] *Auriemma says pre-2008 the client's primary concern was a competitive yield with no onerous restrictions.* "While yield is still important it is secondary to issues such as transparency of the underlying investment portfolio, liquidity and credit risk concerns. [64] "We're seeing some deterioration in their perception of the product, but they're not saying, 'Get me out, They're saying, 'Instead of spending 2.5 seconds on this at our quarterly meeting, let's spend 10 minutes.' There's just a heightened awareness of the product, and more questions." *In comparison to money market funds, stable value funds continue to offer a meaningful yield differential significant to plan sponsors, especially when expressed in terms of opportunity costs. A plan with $20 million in stable value assets yielding as little as 1 percent—well below current average crediting rates—would nonetheless produce $200,000 in annual earnings for plan participants.*

By contrast, a money market fund yielding .01 percent—not uncommon in today's environment—would produce $2,000 in annual earnings. "When you talk about foregone earnings on behalf of participants, sponsors' eyebrows furrow," Auriemma said. *He noted even though expenses for stable value funds have gone up since the financial crisis, mostly due to higher wrap fees, sponsors tend to evaluate the funds in terms of their net yield, which continues to be favorable relative to money market funds. He estimated sponsors would continue to view stable value funds as attractive, relative to money market funds, even if net yields fell as low as 50 basis points.*[65]

PLAN SPONSOR PERSPECTIVE

Keith Watson, director of pension investments for Textron Inc. remarked at the 2015 SVIA Spring Seminar *"Stable value is complicated there are operational risks, wrap capacity and fee issues, participant communications, a whole host of things that come with it. But it's a unique alternative that offers a valuable risk-return profile for our plan participants, and they can't get it anywhere else. There really is no true alternative to stable value."*[66]

Joe Fazzino, senior manager, pension investments, for United Technologies Corp also speaking at the 2015 SVIA Spring Seminar. *"We as an investment staff do believe that this is a gift that's been given to us, to be able to offer our participants par value liquidity, a competitive rate of return, you really cannot find anywhere else in the marketplace,"* Fazzino says. *"So this is something we should continue to take advantage of, even though it may be a bit more burdensome than money market funds."*[67]

Garold Oliver, global pension manager for Hallmark Cards also remarked at the 2015 SVIA Spring Seminar "*Our approach is that nothing really competes with our stable income fund,*" he says. "*Our view at Hallmark is that an allocation to stable value makes sense for everybody, regardless of their age.*"

Some plans sponsors are not as supportive of stable value, primarily because of the complications mentioned above. However, the vast majority continue to use stable value because of its strong risk return tradeoff.

PARTICIPANT DEMAND

Participants continue to love stable value more than any other non-equity asset class. The lure for participants is as a group, DC plan participants tend to be a conservative lot. Writing in the *Financial Analysts Journal*, Saraoglu and Detzler highlight the unique preferences and constraints of individual investors and specifically cite *"preservation of principal"* as a major factor in fund selection.[68] Stable value also adds yield in the form of consistently higher returns than principal-safe money market funds. In fact, stable value offers total returns similar to those of intermediate bonds without the volatility associated with bonds, as illustrated below:

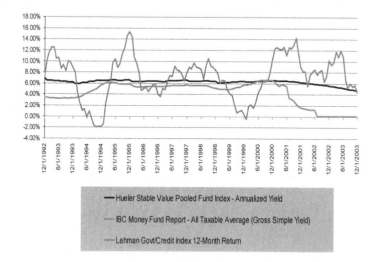

This chart bears repeating in showing the substitutes are either lacking in yield, or have much higher volatility. From 1983 to around 2007, Paul Lipson managed the $3.2 billion stable value fund of the Federal Reserve Employee Benefits System — a fund was extremely popular with the plan's 33,000 participants, drawing an overall allocation of more than 68 percent of the plan. According to Lipson, *"We've delivered a return equal to or greater than that of the Lehman Brothers Aggregate Bond Index over time at one-quarter of the risk."*[69]

INDUSTRY BUY IN

The hybrid quality of stable value has seemed to confuse many of the firms providing asset allocation advice to 401(k) plans and participants. For years, advice providers either left stable value out of asset allocation models or else dumped it with short- to intermediate-term bonds, without capturing the benefit of dampened volatility afforded by stable value's book value guarantee. Major asset allocation advice providers, such as Financial Engines, mPower, and Morningstar's Clear Future, have claimed to bring changes to their allocation models. The results do not bear out they have given full credit of the benefits of stable value in participants' portfolios, including the bond-like returns, money market fund-like volatility, low correlation with equities, and generally lower expense ratios compared to bond funds.[70] The results have been lower allocations to stable value, than if participants had full and accurate data reflected in the models.

Target date funds exclude stable value. While their official reasons mirror those of the advice providers, I think the reason is mostly economic, for most money market and bond mutual funds can charge higher fees than synthetic based stable value in collective investment trusts (CIT). Also there are operational costs of mixing a CIT with mutual funds.

ACCESSING STABLE VALUE

Choosing a stable value option is complicated by the number of different structures the option can take, depending upon the plan's size and the projected stable value assets.

For smaller DC plans under $500 million in assets a pooled fund or collective investment trust (CIT) is probably the best option. Pooled funds theoretically are open to almost all sizes of DC plans (Vanguard has a $1 million minimum), but in reality many plans under $200 million are exclusively mutual funds which eliminates Stable Value solely available in a CIT. If you choose to use a bundled insurance company provider, you will get a general account or insurance company separate account product. Also if a consultant has an insurance license, a general account or separate account product may result in a commission which may not have to be disclosed to the client.

For mid-size DC plans with over $500 million in assets, it is possible to select a single stable value manager. Typically this will be an active fixed income manager of intermediate and long securities with some experience in stable value contracts. Some may market themselves as "managers of managers," where the stable value team may pick and choose among long and intermediate bond managers, either within their own firm or outside of it. Most prevalent is the single-manager fund, which is either a specialty stable value manager or an active fixed income manager, offers numerous key benefits, including maximum control and consistency, reasonable costs, and portability of the stable value fund.[71] For small to medium plans, stable value pooled funds may typically be a good choice, but can vary widely in duration structure, current yields, and crediting rates.

For the largest mega plans (usually $3 billion and up in assets), more sophisticated multi-manager structures have developed. Generally, large plans want to allocate among different underlying bond managers with the objective of accessing different skill sets and excess return diversification, but this requires the ability to objectively allocate between managers.[72] In a multi-manager structure, this allocation role falls primarily falls to the plan sponsor, sometimes with the help of a consultant. Sometimes in multi-manager approaches, the stable value wrapper (an insurance company or bank) can serve as a "master administrator," taking over many of the administrative duties of running a stable value portfolio, thus allowing the sponsor and consultant to focus primarily on strategic allocation decisions.

PUTTING TOGETHER A RFP

The first step in selecting a stable value manager or contract provider is usually constructing a request for proposal to qualified firms, which outlines the structure of the option and the needs of the plan. The RFP structure will determine the type of manager you receive.

Many public plans which currently use insurance company general account or separate account do not bid out the stable value separately. They bid out an overall record keeper who is selected on out of pocket fees. These providers use high internal stable value spreads to enable them to provide what appear to be low bids.

Corporate 401(k) competitive bids are not common. Typically a less formal search process, perhaps led by a consultant or staff is the norm. These searches predominately cover synthetic GICs, and are similar to the search process you would normally see for an intermediate or long bond manager, i.e., with search attributes focused on the "three P's": people, process, and performance, and are Qualified Professional Asset Managers (QPAM) under ERISA.

Unless you plan to let the stable value manager have complete discretion in hiring wrap providers, your process should also include criteria for selecting wrap providers. The criteria should define the wrap provider's qualifications in several key areas: adequate credit quality, standards highlighting stable value experience, reputation, and commitment to the industry; acceptable crediting rate methodology; contract type and terms; soundness of product structure; appropriate administrative systems to support the wrap business and sound operating procedures.[73]

Some of these key areas (e.g., credit quality) are straightforward. Others are fairly subjective in nature (e.g., stable value experience and reputation). For the more subjective areas, you should establish the minimum acceptable standards giving you and the plan sponsor confidence in the provider's wrap expertise. Still others, such as the crediting rate methodology and contract terms, require a fuller understanding since they will directly affect the performance of the fund.

In recent years many independent advisors, who want a good independent synthetic stable value option have to look a little harder to find pooled funds or Collective Investment Trust. Many of the large mutual fund family funds like Fidelity, Vanguard, and T. Rowe many times limit access to plans bundled with their fund families. However by 2015 there is plenty of capacity from pool providers.

CHAPTER SEVEN

BENCHMARKING AND PERFORMANCE

Benchmarking is not as straightforward with Stable Value as with other investment classes in 401(k) and related plans. The most common benchmark is cash or money market index which like stable value low volatility and no down periods. Using a bond benchmark to match the underlying investments in stable value is problematic because its variable returns do not compare directly to the smoothed returns of stable value. Intermediate bond benchmarks and stable value funds while similar over long periods are not relevant in the typical quarterly time periods used.

In 1989 pre-synthetics the Stable Value Investment Association(SVIA) commissioned Ryan Labs to develop a general account GIC for 3 year and 5 year GIC's. [74]

The Stable Value Investment Association (SVIA) commissioned a benchmarking survey in the second quarter of 2003. Of the thirty-five respondents, twenty-six were stable value managers, four were plan sponsors who have an externally managed fund, and five were plan sponsors who manage their fund internally. Respondents were asked how they evaluated book value returns and investment performance, and which investment benchmark(s) they used.

A large majority of respondents — 23 — use money market or other cash-based indexes to benchmark stable value's book value. Seven respondents use the Constant Maturity Treasury (CMT) index; five use a GIC index; four use a wrapped fixed income index; two use the Hueler Index of Pooled Funds; and two use a long term market value index.[75] This survey from 2003 has not changed dramatically into 2015 as no one standard has emerged.

But using money market funds as the predominant performance benchmark for stable value funds presents another challenge: stable value managers consistently beat money market returns by wide margins during most markets. Because of this, plan sponsors and consultants have looked for more ways to distinguish between stable value managers. Many have looked at market value results for greater insight into how their managers are performing *Stable Times* quotes Vicky Paradis, a vice president with stable value manager JP Morgan Fleming Asset Management, as saying: *"Historically, the way everyone evaluated stable value funds was to look at their book value performance results. That is and always will be an effective way to measure a fund's success at meeting participant expectations. But it's not meaningful in evaluating a manager, because a book-value return series is a smoothed series that is hugely affected by things managers cannot control, such as cash flow timing, portfolio guidelines, and portfolio funding dates. We need a measure that highlights decisions that managers can control."*[76] In the same article, Greg DeForrest, a fixed income specialist in the global manager research group at Callan Associates, an investment consulting firm, maintains whatever benchmark is finally chosen, the job of benchmarking stable value managers will be easier once they are reporting total-return results.

DeForrest's firm compares the market value returns of wrapped bond portfolios to common bond market indices, such as the Lehman Aggregate and the Lehman Intermediate Aggregate indices. In the case of stable value funds holding other assets, such as traditional GICs, Callan will compare their book value performance with peers, or, in some cases, against blended benchmarks it creates using a variety of bond indices of both intermediate and short duration.[77]

After 2008 most stable value managers moved to intermediate or shorter portfolios with less risk. Barclays (who took over the Lehman bond indices) in 2010 developed the Stable Income Market Index (SIMI) with the underlying bonds more conservative than even their intermediate aggregate indices. [78] The index is comprised of a low-risk blend of asset classes from within the BarCap U.S. Aggregate Bond Index, focusing on shorter maturities and providing diversified exposure to debt from the government, credit and structured sectors of the bond market. Stable Income Market Index (SIMI) Benchmark Allocation Government Credit 1-5 Year 65.0% MBS 15 Year Fixed Rate 25.0% CMBS AAA 1-6 Years 5.0% ABS Credit Cards (AAA) 2.5% ABS Autos (AAA) 2.5%. [79] A comparison (May 2015) to the US Aggregate show it with a much lower duration of 2.67 vs 5.56, and a much lower yield at 1.20% compared to 2.28%. [80]

Mercer Investment Consulting, from the *Stable Times* Article says it continues to rely on book value returns when evaluating stable value managers for its plan sponsor clients, according to Phil Suess, a Chicago-based principal with the firm and head of its Mercer Insurance Group, who was also interviewed for the *Stable Times*: *"The two things we do focus on when we look at stable value — and it probably comes across to some as rather simplistic — we look at it in the context of determining what this vehicle needs to provide in order to be a viable option under a defined contribution plan. And the thing we focus on there is [that] it needs to provide a meaningful premium above money market instruments. Our expectation is that to the extent we have a stable value fund, we're going to be able to earn 100 to 150 basis points above money market funds over time — a three-to-five-year period. The second thing we focus on, and it's not necessarily as meaningful, we essentially take the median of the Hueler universe and share that with clients as kind of a benchmark as to what other stable value funds are doing."* [81]

Due to the lack of a secondary market for stable value contracts and the fact participants receive book value returns, the CFA Institutes Global Investment Performance Standards (GIPS) has specifically identified GICs as assets excluded from the mark to market requirements. This allows stable value managers to claim performance presentation compliance.[82] However many of the underlying bond portfolios in synthetic stable value can provide typical GIPS compliant performance. Valuing the benefit responsive feature of high liquidity at the participant level and low liquidity at the plan level is a challenge.[83] The industry predominately views the crediting rate reported to participants as the most important number.

Whether or not you look at book value or market value when evaluating the performance of stable value managers and/or contract providers, it's important not to focus purely on numbers. The performance dimensions of liquidity management and risk management count as well. Here, the questions to answer include: how does a manager control credit exposures and deal with liquidity issues? For synthetic GICs, the questions include: how does the plan-level investment management agreement compare to the investment guidelines in the wrap contract? (Most wrap contracts have distinct investment policy requirements.) It's important, too, to evaluate the manager's liquidity and risk management capabilities because there is typically a trade-off between the level of the crediting rate and the stability of the crediting rate. For example, a lower credit quality, longer duration portfolio will generally have a higher initial crediting rate than a higher quality, shorter duration portfolio, but the crediting will also tend to be much more volatile.

CHAPTER EIGHT

FIXED INCOME UNDERLYING INVESTMENTS

Stable value is based on fixed income investments. In the stable value crediting model the yield is directly linked to the crediting rate, but it also takes into effect the market appreciation and depreciation of the bond portfolio in the formula. In the insurance world, yield is still primary, but in the money management world, where many of the synthetic managers operate, total return is the main metric. Spreads to treasury or spreads to LIBOR are other measures of yield and return to look at.

The 1998 Handbook of Stable value by Fabozzi et al. gave historic 20 year returns on Stable Value around 40 basis points less than Intermediate Bonds but over 120 basis points more per year than Money Market. [84] It referenced 3 objectives for stable value funds: safety, liquidity and return. The need is to provide daily liquidity to participants at the lowest possible cost. The technical term for liquidity for participants specifically is benefit responsive. In a 401k context, stable value is benefit responsive giving the same full liquidity as money market to individual participants. This historic figure includes all three types of stable value, synthetic, separate and general account.

SYNTHETIC FIXED INCOME INVESTMENTS

The best way to look at synthetic stable value, is to think of the intermediate bond index with a wrapper over top of it smoothing returns and preventing negative returns. The underlying bond fund is owned by the plan and the wrap makes up any difference if the fund is underwater. The long term intermediate bond fund return and the stable value fund should differ primarily by the synthetic GIC or wrap fee. Historically wrap fees were insignificant 6-8 basis points pre-2008, but are up to over 20 bps post 2008.

In recent years US Treasury yields, are at historic lows. The bonds underlying stable value like most other bond funds are driven by the Treasury yield curve. Part of the stable value pickup in return over money market comes from an upwardly sloping yield curve. As of 5/1/2015 the 1 year US Treasury stood at 0.25%, while the 5 year US Treasury stood at 1.50%. While the spread seems small at 1.25% or 125 basis points, it could also been seen as 6 times the yield. [85]

In 2010 Barclays Capital launched its Stable Income Market Index (SIMI), the first performance benchmark designed specifically for the underlying bond portfolio within stable value funds. The index is comprised of a low-risk blend of asset classes from within the BarCap U.S. Aggregate Bond Index, focusing on shorter maturities and providing diversified exposure to debt from the government, credit and structured sectors of the bond market.

Stable Income Market Index (SIMI) Benchmark Allocation Government Credit 1-5 Year 65.0% MBS 15 Year Fixed Rate 25.0% CMBS AAA 1-6 Years 5.0% ABS Credit Cards (AAA) 2.5% ABS Autos (AAA) 2.5%. [86] This index is appropriate for synthetics but the underlying portfolios of insurance company general account have much lower credit and much higher duration.

The standard for bond funds underlying synthetic stable value is 100% investment grade fixed income securities similar to the index with no leverage. The Department of Labor (DOL), in 2005, fined Circle Trust $8.8 million for using non-rated securities (i.e. alternative hedge funds) in a synthetic stable value portfolio. [87] One notable exception to using unrated non-securities is the subject of current litigation against JP Morgan's synthetic stable value. [88]

Another measure of underlying investments is a classification system of the Financial Accounting Standards Board (FASB). FASB 157 classifies assets as Level 1, Level 2, and Level 3. All government bonds are in Level 1, but some of the lower rated corporate and non-government MBS and ABS moved into Level II after 2008. The underlying assets in stable value funds have been predominantly classified as Level 1, with some, perhaps 10% in Level 2. Private Mortgage Placements, hedge funds and other non-securities are Level 3 assets and never appropriate for synthetic stable value.

Typical fixed income guidelines are established by Synthetic GIC contracts. Duration limits are probably the most critical. Post 2008 many SV plans have duration in the 2 to 2.5 year range. However pre 2008 durations were typically over 3 and some in the 4 year range with a few even higher if pegged to the duration of a Lehman Aggregate Bond Index the predominant fixed income benchmark for pensions. More typical have been the Intermediate indexes, but post 2008 even shorter than the intermediate is not uncommon. This is driven by the historical norm of over 60% of the yield curve spread is captured in the 1 year to 5 year maturity range. [89]

Credit quality is also important. Current post 2008 synthetics have demanded all the underlying investments be investment grade securities. Pre-2008 there had been exceptions with small allocations to rated assets like high yield.

Diversification between fixed income sectors has been extremely important post 2008 as many of the poor performers were caused by overweights into non-government Mortgage Backed Securities (MBS) and certain Asset Backed Securities (ABS). Pre-2008 the weights of the then Lehman indices, but since most fixed income managers thought they could add value by underweighting Treasuries and Agencies many allowed higher allocations to Corporates, MBS and ABS. For example many had corporate bond limited to 50% when the index (LehAG) limit was 20%. Also many had MBS up to 75% and ABS limits to 50%, but these guidelines have tightened post 2008,[90]

FIXED INCOME INVESTMENTS IN GENERAL ACCOUNT AND SEPARATE ACCOUNT.

For General Account and Separate Accounts the returns of the underlying investments are not a pass through but commingled with many other accounts on the insurance company balance sheet and sometimes matched with the underlying returns of a list of assets to give the appearance of ownership and pass through returns. They are also allowed to use leverage which increases the insurance company profits but is typically not passed on to policy holders.

General Account and Separate Accounts can offer higher current yields than synthetics.

Riskier underlying fixed income investments with higher duration, lower overall credit ratings, high yield, private debt, illiquid real estate debt are most prevalent. In the General Account limited equity risk up to 10%+ equities, hedge funds, real estate equity, private equity are allowed. Levels of leverage can be employed in both separate and general accounts depending on the state regulations.

According to a 2012 Blue Prarie study Separate Account have on average duration 171% of diversified synthetic based stable value (4.73 vs. 2.76) and this correlated directly with the performance claims that insurance companies have used to increase business.

An October 2014 term sheet from the Lincoln Financial Stable value General Account quotes a 2.25% annual rate. The underlying investments driving this rate are extremely different from the Barclays Capital launched its Stable Income Market Index (SIMI). The duration is not listed but it could be higher than perhaps even the separate accounts of 4.73 years. The corporate bonds held at 70% are probably three times or more than SIMI indicating a lower credit quality. The general accounts holding of 5% in US Treasury and governments is much lower than the indices. Over 8% is in "other" not fixed income including stocks and alternatives. 9% is in illiquid commercial mortgages. Neither of these asset classes totaling 17% are included in the SIMI.

Liquidity is important for 401(k) plans. There have been moves to allow more illiquid investments but some have resulted in legal action [91]like the Principal real estate option. [92] Liquidity issues of general account products have prompted some fiduciaries to not use them even if it is the only form of stable value available for especially smaller accounts.

CHAPTER NINE

DEFINING STABLE VALUE RISKS

In 2008 there was a major disruption in the stable value market with a Synthetic GIC shortage. This prompted some larger plans to drop stable value, and allowed some of the older forms of stable value from the 90's and 80's to regain some market share. Missing was a way to measure the structural risk differences of the wrap or insurance segments of stable value investment options in 401(k) s and related U.S. Defined contribution plans. We do have credit ratings on the pieces of the insurance structure, and a rating on the underlying securities, but they do not get to the real distinctions of risk between the newer and older stable value options. I came up with the risk scoring idea in a December 2012 whitepaper since I wanted to come up with a way to differentiate the insurance part of the stable value structure. [93]

There are three basic categories of stable value: (1) The original *General Account* or *traditional GIC*, (2) the *Insurance Company Separate Account GIC* and (3) the *Synthetic GIC*, sometimes known as a *wrap*.[94] In my consulting practice I have developed a scoring system to quantify the risk difference between all of these categories, and the effects of diversification within these categories, and even mixing and matching different structures within the same stable value fund.

The definitive and only major book published was The Handbook of Stable Value Investments edited by Frank Fabozzi in 1998. Chapter 14 on Evaluating Wrap Provider Credit Risk in Synthetic GIC's by Jacqueline Griffin quantifies the credit risk of a General Account is ten times in magnitude of a Synthetic.[95] This chapter did not look at Insurance Company Separate Account products or explore the effects of diversification. Chapter 16 does look at pricing general account stable value risks.

The U.S. pension trade press on stable-value funds has focused primarily on the Synthetic GIC wrap-type products that have dominated the large-plan market in the last ten years. *Pension & Investments* recently described this type of stable-value fund: *They typically invest in high-quality, short-maturity—usually under five years—corporate and government bonds, mortgage-backed securities and asset-backed securities, and are protected by so-called wrap contracts*[96] However, small to mid size ERISA plans and all sizes of non-ERISA public and non-profit plans have continued to use both General Account (GA) and Insurance Company Separate Account (SA) products.

The financial crisis created a wrap shortage in the Synthetic GIC market. Unlike the other GIC markets, the Synthetic market had evolved prior to 2008 into 2/3's of the players were not insurance companies but banks. All of these large global banks were affected by the crisis and many dropped out of the Synthetic GIC business. However, since the crisis some insurance companies have entered the Synthetic market while others looked to gain back market share from the 80's and 90's for their highly profitable SA and GA products.

With the other two categories—insurance company Separate Account and General Account GICs—the pension plan does not own any securities but owns solely a contract with an insurance company. Mega 401(k) plans (Fortune 100) subject to ERISA abandoned General Account GICs 20 years ago after defaults by Executive Life and Confederation Life in 1992. Large ERISA plans for the most part abandoned insurance company Separate Account stable value a decade ago because of concerns the single-entity credit risk could be a fiduciary liability. [97]

The crisis provided in AIG is good example since under different subsidiaries they offered all three versions of stable value. In 2008 Federal Reserve Chairman Ben Bernanke said that *"workers whose 401(k) plans had purchased $40 billion of insurance from AIG against the risk that their stable-value funds would decline in value would have seen that insurance disappear."*[98] These 3 different AIG structures would have experienced vastly different outcomes if AIG had been allowed to fail. Even with the bailout many plans wanted out of AIG and those with Synthetic GIC's were for the most part able to replace them with other company Synthetic GIC's at little or no cost. This risk scoring system hopes to better measure risk and help predict the differences in these outcomes.

In an article on DOL fee disclosure rules, I document General Account and Separate Account stable value products tend to mask both risk and costs.[99] Since General and Separate Account stable-value assets are on the balance sheet of the insurance company, this creates an inherent conflict between the fiduciary care of pension investors and company shareholders.[100] This increased regulatory and litigation risk, while not specifically measured in my scoring system, I feel is material.

GENERAL ACCOUNT (GA) RISKS

The National Association of Government Defined Contribution Administrators, Inc. (NAGDCA) which represents large State and City public DC plans in September 2010 created a brochure with this characterization of General Account stable value: *Due to the fact that the plan sponsor does not own the underlying investments, the portfolio holdings, performance, risk, and management fees are generally not disclosed. This limits the ability of plan sponsors to compare returns with other SVFs [stable-value funds]. It also makes it nearly impossible for plan sponsors to know the fees (which can be increased without disclosure) paid by participants in these funds—a critical component of a fiduciary's responsibility.*[101] In May 2010, the *Wall Street Journal* reported: *Amid the shortage of wrap insurance, though, some firms are seizing an opportunity to reintroduce older types of stable-value products that are backed by a single insurer and carry considerable risks. OneAmerica Financial Partners Inc.'s American United Life Insurance Co., for example, last month launched a stable-value product backed by its own General-Account assets. In such products, investors are taking on the risk that this single issuer could go belly up.* [102] The regulatory limits on leverage are vague within these accounts and can vary widely by state and firm. There is a growing consensus in the Plan Sponsor community

General Account stable value is hard to justify from a risk/return standpoint.

In my 2011 article in IFEBP's Benefits Magazine I tell plan sponsors to ask the following five questions:

- Is my insurance company too big to fail?
- Which state regulates my contract? How solid is this regulation?
- Do I want to own the underlying assets or a piece of paper from an insurance company during the next financial crisis?
- Am I comfortable taking single-entity credit risk when better diversified options are available?
- Is the insurance company accepting fiduciary liability?[103]

Insurance companies like to claim they have significant regulatory reserves, but they are reluctant to detail the amounts. They also claim that there is significant coverage from the state guaranty associations which vary widely and cover health and all types of other insurance. Given the lack of transparency and proof otherwise, many of these state guaranty associations are underfunded for severe events. The market does not think much of these state reserve claims, as credit default swaps for most of the leading insurance companies have traded at over 200 basis points. This leaves the justification for feeling safe with a single insurer is the insurance company backing the GA stable value option is "too big to fail" and has an implied government guarantee. This case can be made with the 3 insurance companies Metlife, AIG, and Prudential recently named as SIFI's or "too big to fail." [104] However, do to the fact many of these insurance companies are actively trying to get away from SIFI status with its higher capital requirements leading to less profit, makes it hard to make long term commitments based on them being too big to fail.

INSURANCE COMPANY SEPARATE ACCOUNT (SA) RISKS

Stable value in an insurance company Separate Account was sold after the 1992 defaults as an improvement on General Account for larger plans and was widely adopted in the 90's. Most of the largest ERISA plans had moved on to Synthetics by 2000. However, insurance companies continue to sell Separate Account stable value as being similar to a Synthetic wrapped stable-value fund to all sizes of public 457 plans and small to mid-size ERISA 401(k) plans.

In reality a Separate Account gives the *appearance* the plan owns a unique portfolio, but in the end, all the plan has is a piece of paper—a claim on the assets of the insurance company. A good example comes from a NAGDCA publication: *"However due to the fact the assets are segregated, the plan sponsor **may** have additional transparency regarding portfolio holdings, performance and fees.*[105] The critical word is "may" at the insurance company's discretion. Again they may not, or give some transparency some time, but when times are bad shut it off. If you want to test this term ask them to put in writing you have full transparency on holdings, performance and fees at all times. In good times Separate Account looks like a Synthetic, but in bad times it can convert to be like General Account in liquidity.

While managing Insurance Company Separate Account Index product to DB ERISA plans most would limit total exposure to our insurance company 5%, which was their exposure to any one credit. I made the argument to the DB plans the 5% limit would be appropriate for General Account product, but they should be able to go to 10% limit on Separate Account. In the end the DB plans could not get to that level of distinction in credit and liquidity risk between General Account and Separate Account product, because they felt during a crisis the distinction would disappear.

In even getting DB plans to take 5% in Separate Account product I reviewed and explained detailed legal opinions on what would happen in a default situation. My reading was in the event of default, Separate Accounts would be above General Account, but would be classified as a Class 2 priority. Class one would be payroll etc. of employees, while General Account would be in the 3rd or 4th tier. Within class 2 the Separate Account would rank equal or pari passu with the claims of life insurance policyholders. However a bankruptcy judge could control the order in the Class 2 to put all of the policy holders ahead of the Separate Account holders. In a bankruptcy situation while you are ahead in line of General Account products it could still be months or years before you could get your money out of a Separate Account. Given this research it amazes me the amount of single entity credit risk and liquidity risk especially public plans are willing to take in an Insurance Company Separate Account. [106]

In my scoring system insurance company Separate Account (SA) product are penalized severely for a lack of liquidity. The regulatory limits on leverage are vague within these accounts and can vary widely by state and firm. In the worst situations liquidity is king. While Separate Account products many times show plans statements with individual securities like a Synthetic, I think this is misleading because it cannot pass the following test: Ask the insurance company to put in writing if it goes into default or is even downgraded, the company will wire "the plan's" securities to the plan within five days or five weeks or five months. My experience is they will always refuse, proving you do not have liquidity when you probably need it the most.

SYNTHETIC GIC RISKS

Diversification between fixed income sectors has been extremely important post 2008 as many of the poor performers were caused by over weights into Mortgage Backed Securities (MBS) and certain Asset Backed Securities (ABS). The guidelines looked at the weights of the then Lehman bond indices, but since most fixed income managers thought they could add value by underweighting Treasuries and Agencies many had high allocations to Corporates, MBS and ABS. Many had much looser actual guidelines with Corporates allowed as high as 50% when the AG index limit was 20%. Many had MBS up to 75% and ABS limits 50% or so buy many have tightened post 2008 to levels closer to the index.[107]

CHAPTER TEN

STABLE VALUE RISK APPLICATIONS

SYNTHETIC GIC RISKS- MYTHS

There is a myth that diversified synthetic stable value somehow has more risks than other fixed income options for 401k plans with near identical underlying investments. This myth is perpetuated primarily by competitors whose products have high fees and either higher risks or lower returns. An excellent 2014 paper by Vanguard busts the myth on the vulnerability of stable value to spikes in interest rates. [108]

From a Fiduciary Risk standpoint, diversified synthetic based stable value is the superior fixed income choice for DC plans. Alternatives including money market funds, bond funds, and general and insurance company separate account products are inferior from a risk/return perspective. However with many plans under $200 million access issues involving plan structure eliminates synthetic options, and these second best alternatives are your only option.

Money market funds in 2015 have beat back a challenge by the SEC on principal protection regulations, but their bigger problem is near zero rates. In a case against Southern California Edison plaintiffs claim SCE damaged them by offering a lower return money market instead of stable value.[109] Even though that judge did not rule on this specific argument, I think it is likely that someone in the future will sue a plan terminating stable value to go into a money market fund over the lower returns.

Bond funds, because of their market value fluctuations, have never been popular with 401(k) participants. A significant portion of their market share is concentrated in the plans which do not have a diversified synthetic stable value option. While participants expect fluctuations in their stock funds, they tend to prefer stability in their fixed income. The only real difference in long term performance between bonds and synthetic stable value is the wrap fees.

Insurance company general and separate account products attempted to use the wrap shortage to attempt to turn the clock back to the 90's and recover what they lost from synthetics. While they have successfully lobbied the DOL to exempt these products from the new 408(b) fee disclosure requirements, I do not think it will hold up in court over time. In some of the disclosure documents I reviewed the general account stable value reports 0% in fees.

Currently these higher risk and higher fee bundled products will appear to have lower fees (and higher returns) compared to a diversified low risk low fee product like the Vanguard Stable Value collective trust. While they have lobbied the DOL they have 0 fees (so far successfully) these same publicly traded insurance companies will brag to stock analysts how they make 200 basis points in profit on this 401(k) business without disclosing it.[110] Hopefully it will not take an insurance company default to expose these hidden profits.

Wrap capacity issues are over but there is still some leftover hype pushed by competitors. A May 2012 P&I Conference Call called the turn with a positive outlook for wrap capacity. [111] Karl Tourville of Galliard said we have gone from *"10 active wrap providers in 2008 to 16 in 2012 and that we have $30 to $40 billion in additional wrap capacity. "* New wrappers in 2012 were Bank of Tokyo – Mitsubishi and RGA – reinsurance out of St. Louis.

Vanguard, in their paper **"Stable value pooled funds: Scenarios for rising rates and cash outflows"** puts two hypothetical cash-withdrawal scenarios to the test. The report states: *"Relatively low volatility makes stable value funds attractive to many defined contribution plans. In general, such funds have performed well during past market crises. However, in the current low-interest-rate environment, some investors and contract providers worry that adverse market conditions and cash flow* *activity could impair fund performance."* [112] The report shows how well stable value will hold up under most realistic interest rate scenarios, and should put some fears to rest.

Many of these myths are perpetuated by a lack of understanding and bias by financial advisors who dominate the small and mid-size portions of the 401(k) markets. In several articles I am quoted in, some of the advisors are incomprehensible when they talk about stable value. [113] Some advisors are able to capture more commissions and other revenues through insurance products than they can in a diversified synthetic fund.

TIMING RISKS – COMPETING FUNDS- EQUITY WASH

Market timing also can be a potential risk to stable value fund participants. As with any investment fund, more sophisticated stable value investors can attempt to execute trades benefiting them at the expense of remaining participants. This is particularly true in multi-option plans where stable value is offered alongside "competing fund" options, such as money market funds or brokerage windows. A "competing fund" is any fund with the same or lower duration than stable value may present arbitrage opportunities because of the difference in market prices. To circumvent the arbitrage risk posed by competing funds, most stable value providers require an "equity wash" for plans offering competing funds alongside stable value. An equity wash requires funds transferred out of stable value to a competing fund be held for up to ninety days in an equity fund before the trade is completed. This effectively eliminates any incentive for arbitrage.[114]

THE SCORING SYSTEM

I, in my company Stable Value Consultants, have developed a scoring system based primarily on my experience as an officer for an insurance company, pricing and underwriting all three types of stable value in combination with basic diversification principles and previously published basic risk principals. My scoring metric goes from 0 using a Government risk free option (G fund in the Thrift Savings plan) to a high of 100 for a single entity General Account product. I give a single entity Insurance Company Separate Account a 65 giving it significantly less credit and liquidity risk than General Account. I rate a one single Synthetic wrapper (over a 100% investment grade fixed income security portfolio) with a 25 primarily for its lower liquidity risk. I think this scoring system is conservative given I could have justified a score of 250 for single entity General Account based on credit risk ratios set out the Handbook of Stable Value,[115] and have not included the increased regulatory and litigation risk I document in other articles.[116]

As does stock diversification, getting away from single entity going from one to two is a huge reduction in risk, two to three big, three to four less big and so on. With two wrappers my Synthetic number drops to 15, with three Synthetics 10, and 4 Synthetics 8, as there are diminishing returns in diversification. With over 4 Synthetic names adding any number of wrappers subtracts a point in total, because of the ease of substitution with synthetic providers.

In practice recently Insurance Company Separate Accounts have been mixed with Synthetic wraps. This risk can be acceptable in small amounts as my scoring system gives the first 5% no negative effect, the next 5% adds 5 points etc. This should be especially helpful in comparing stable value collective investment trust (CIT) structures. It is my estimate most of the best stable value collective funds as well as most Fortune 50 corporate plans will have scores of less than 30 with many below 15.

There are prudent ways to structure all 3 types of stable value for plans. However many structures today that are not ideal and subject plans to unneeded fiduciary risk. This risk scoring system gives some scale and measurability to the wide variety of risk structures within stable value.

We do have credit ratings on the pieces of the insurance structure, and a rating on the underlying securities, but they do not get to the real distinctions of risk between the newer and older stable value options. This is my first attempt at scoring funds, so I decided to do it with Collective Investment Trusts. These were readily available scores. All of the 100% Separate Account on one balance sheet like Met which includes many Prudential and Great West Products would score a 65. All of the 100% General Account with one company products like Lincoln, would include products from TIAA-CREF and Nationwide all would score 100. A recent Blue Prairie report showed assets under separate accounts had close to twice the duration of those in synthetics, and have looser guidelines on high yield and even allow some equity. This risk structure measure should be able to explain most of the yield differences in stable value products today.

CHAPTER ELEVEN

REGULATIONS & LEGAL CASES

REGULATORS

Stable value for the most part is lightly regulated because it historically has had few problems and, in addition, falls in many grey areas of the regulatory scheme of both Federal and State Laws.

All corporate 401(k) plans come under the jurisdiction of the US Department of Labor under the ERISA act. However 401(k)'s sponsored by state and local governments as well as similar 457 plans are exempt from ERISA. Many non-profits who use 401(k) and 403(b) plans are mostly exempt from ERISA. Whether stable value providers are ERISA fiduciaries depends on the circumstances. [117]

Almost all stable value products are regulated and governed by State Insurance Laws. Many states however adopt standards if the National Association of Insurance Commissioners called NAIC model contracts. [118] However many states are more lenient on capital and other requirements. This allows Stable value providers to shop for states with the least regulation. New York is known as having the toughest state insurance laws, so most insurance providers try to avoid writing contracts out of New York.

The U.S. Securities and Exchange Commission (SEC) decided in 2004 it did not want to regulate Stable Value Mutual funds and essentially forced the closure of 3 funds with excellent track records. Most underlying fixed income managers of synthetic stable value are under SEC jurisdiction as Registered Investment Advisors. Many large insurance companies are publicly held and thus regulated by the SEC. Dodd-Frank has suggested there may be future regulation from **Commodity Futures Trading Commission (CFTC)**.

Stable Value Pooled funds or Collective Investment Trusts (CITs) are not regulated by the SEC and the Investment Company Act of 1940 but most are regulated by the Office of the Comptroller of the Currency ("OCC")[119] and subject to oversight by the Internal Revenue Service ("IRS") and the Department of Labor ("DOL"). However not all are regulated by the OCC with a significant number regulated by state banking commissioners and laws.

It is still not known what types of regulation stable value will face due to Dodd-Frank Wall Street Reform and Consumer Protection Act of 2010. Steve Kolocotronis, the vice president and associate general counsel for Fidelity Investments spent an entire session on this issue at the Stable Value Investment Association (SVIA) 2015 Spring Seminar. [120]

The Dodd-Frank Act asked the SEC and the CFTC to study whether stable value contracts should be regulated like financial swaps. The study was scheduled to be completed by 2011 but as of summer 2015 has not been heard from. Kolocotronis reminded SVIA seminar participants until regulators do act, wrap contracts continue to fall outside the purview of Dodd-Frank.[121]

Competitors have worked overtime to try to spread myths about stable value to Washington regulators. The SEC-CFTC swap initiative was one area of concern. I shared my opinion with both the SEC and CFTC as did others. As of 2015 it looks like they will not do nothing to harm stable value contracts...

I experienced another attack with the GAO attacking stable value withdrawal assumptions. I spent time with GAO staff, and Senator Kohl's staff and it has not become a major issue.[122]

LEGAL CASES

Cases in the 401(k) area can drag on for 5 to 10 years and a few have looked at stable value issues.

Originally filed in 2007 the case Abbott et.al vs. Lockheed Martin settled in early 2015 for $62 million. Of this $62 million in damages 63% of this came from a subpar stable value option. My understanding was the stable value option was in name only and in fact was a much lower yielding money market option. The damages awarded were based on the Stable Value Fund unit's underperformance relative to the Hueler First Source Index. [123]

Another case involved employees of CIGNA which was acquired by Prudential. Prudential/CIGNA paid a settlement of $35 million for unreasonable fees. This document from the case linked from the blog FRA Plan Tools summarizes.[124]

Broadly, Plaintiffs contend that their employer CIGNA Corporation and its officers, employees, and subsidiaries operated Plaintiffs' 401(k) Plan not for the exclusive benefit of Plan participants as ERISA requires, but instead as a profit center for CIGNA's business by taking unreasonable fees from participant accounts, using its own funds, never putting Plan services out for competitive bids, and engaging in prohibited transactions with Plan assets. Indeed, Plaintiff's 401(k) Plan was the flagship and largest 401(k) plan in CIGNA's Retirement Division, which it sold in April 2004 to Prudential Financial Inc. for over $2 billion. Despite their retirement assets providing seed capital for CIGNA's retirement business, Plan participants received none of the profit CIGNA received from the sale. A vital component of that sale was a secret "gentlemen's agreement" between CIGNA and Prudential under which CIGNA secretly committed to keep Prudential on as the fee-earning fiduciary of the Plan for at least three years after the sale, to get a higher sale price for itself and to ensure Prudential would benefit from the profits generated by the unreasonable 401(k) Plan fees paid by participants. Even though CIGNA remained a Plan fiduciary, it allowed Prudential to continue taking unreasonable and prohibited fees from Plan assets.

Prudential, which became a fiduciary to the Plan upon closing the sale, commenced doing the same thing CIGNA had done – using its own funds, not putting services out for bids, taking grossly excessive fees, determining what its own fees are, and engaging in prohibited transactions with Plan assets.

FRA goes on to say a significant part of plaintiffs' claims had to do with an investment of over $1 billion in stable value assets invested in Cigna's general account, a practice the plaintiffs alleged was imprudent and self-serving. [125] This general account product was assumed by Prudential which admitted secret hidden spread fees of over 200 basis Points in these type products when touting profits to stock analysts.[126]

Liquid securities are the overwhelming investment in all 401(k) and especially stable value. A few exceptions exist and some have resulted in legal action [127]like the Principal real estate option. [128]

There have been a number of cases surrounding the Synthetic based JP Morgan Stable Value funds, over their underlying investments, primarily JP Morgan proprietary funds and assets and Reuters reports it is also being investigated by the US. Department of Labor. [129]

Reuters writes JPMorgan Stable Asset Income Fund has invested as much as 13 percent in private mortgage debt underwritten and rated by the bank itself, according to investment documents reviewed by Reuters.[130] In November 2008, the market to book value of JPMorgan's stable value portfolio for a number of 401(k) plans fell as low as 86.55 percent, according to people familiar with the situation.[131]

This Stable Value issue accounted for $128 million of the American Century $373 Million Arbitration settlement against JP Morgan.[132] This has led to at least 3 additional cases which are ongoing.[133] One case is ERISA based and another is based on state security law. [134]

One general account stable value lawsuit is ongoing Teets v. Great-West Life but there is not much information available at the time of publication. After settlements in the Prudential and Lockheed Martin cases it is highly likely there will be more Stable Value litigation.

CHAPTER TWELVE

SYNTHETIC GIC CONTRACT RISK MANAGEMENT

For stable value portfolios using synthetic GICs, credit risk is low since the plan retains asset ownership and the wrap contract covers solely the difference between market value and book value, i.e., the wrap provider must pay if total book value withdrawals exceed the market value of the portfolio's underlying securities. Typically, market-to-book value shortfalls range from one to five percent. Because of this, it has been demonstrated the default risk of synthetic GICs is less than one-tenth of a traditional GIC issued by the same company.[135]

Many stable value managers, however, still opt to diversify with two or more wrappers and may limit the credit quality of the wrapper to a minimum A or AA. The main reason to diversify is a number of wrappers enter and exit the business on a regular basis. What typically happens when a wrapper leaves the business (or in an extreme case fails) is the other wrappers in the plan will agree to take on their share of the wrap.

I want to focus on two hypothetical and rare negative outcomes which plans should be aware of. The worst is loss of book value coverage which can force a write down and expose the plan to potential liability. The second, extended termination, is a forced wind down usually by the synthetic GIC wrap provider lowering the crediting rate to participants to near zero but avoids the liability of a loss. Both of these outcomes until 2008 were considered extremely unlikely.

Morningstar in a August 2015 article addresses risks of layoffs, mergers, and bankruptcy of the plan sponsor. " *In the event that an employer goes bankrupt, the plan sponsor and the protection provider generally have time to figure out a plan to cover the assets in the stable-value fund so that the participants can continue to transact at book value, according to the SVIA. But this did not happen in the case of Lehman Brothers in 2008, due to the scale of the bankruptcy (the largest in U.S. history) and the swiftness at which it proceeded. Lehman's bankruptcy led to huge withdrawals from the stable-value fund in Lehman Brothers' retirement plan, forcing the plan sponsor to have to sell underlying securities at a discount. The stable-value fund in Lehman Brothers' plan had a return of negative 1.7% in December 2008 but still managed an annual return for 2008 of 2%, according to the SVIA.[136]"*

While I agree with the stable value industry consensus Lehman is an isolated event due to the rapid nature of the bankruptcy, there still could be other company or plan related events leading to a loss.

I see four major potential causes for concern:
1. Downgrade or defaults of wrappers
2. Investment under performance due to subprime and other asset backed securities
3. Major wrapper capacity issues which have led to a doubling of fees.
4. Plan related events or employer directed events.

Many plans have more than one of these issues which increases the likelihood of a negative outcome.

REACTIONS IN 2008

One major stable value manager State Street Global Advisors (SSGA) investments in underlying bond funds were hit hard in 2007 and early 2008 by sub-prime and other related home mortgage securities. To avoid extended termination by the wrappers SSGA voluntarily contributed $160 million in January 2008 and an additional $450 million in the fourth quarter of 2008 in a negotiated settlement with the wrappers.[137]

Another stable value manager Merrill Lynch also chose to make its investors whole. Former Merrill Lynch executive Sallie Krawcheck recently cited this in a story entitled "7 Business Leaders Share How They Solved The Biggest Moral Dilemmas Of Their Careers. " [138]

"There were two options, one of which was to say tough luck to the Walmart employees who owned the Stable Value Fund or to put money in, in order to increase the [fund's] value."

While State Street and Merrill Lynch did the right thing and made investors whole, one stable value manager J.P. Morgan has not, which is covered in the current lawsuit section of chapter 11.

BACKGROUND

The wrapper protects the principal and passes through the performance of the underlying portfolio to plan participants. Plans either use the synthetic approach on a separate investment account or they are in a Stable Value pooled fund which is primarily synthetics but in some cases has a diversified portfolio of traditional GICs as well.

Stable Value or book value accounting works because it looks at valuation from the standpoint of the individual 401k participant, so a participant gets the same daily liquidity he can get from a money market fund or other option. The participant gets this valuation at book value which is equal to his deposits plus a credited rate and never gets a loss over any measured (mostly quarterly but sometimes monthly) period. So for the individual his market value is the book value, and thus the underlying portfolio market value is allowed to deviate from the book value as long as a wrapper is insuring the difference. This was originally confirmed at the request of FASB in AICPA Statement of Position 94-4 and reaffirmed in 2006 with FSP AAG INV-a. Accordingly, author Paul Donahue has argued a wrap is, by definition, an insurance contract not a derivative.[139] This is an important distinction because, pursuant to SOP 94-4, insurance contracts allow stable value book value accounting treatment, while derivatives are subject to more rigid mark to market accounting.[140]

Wrappers provide this cushion over market fluctuations, first because over time they know markets are somewhat in equilibrium over time and participants, because of tax and other issues do not withdraw all of their money out over short periods of time. They also write provisions in their contracts to protect themselves from events outside their assumptions. They all have clauses on Extended Termination, which allow them to exit the contract over typically a 2 to 4 year period.

CAUSES- WRAPPER DOWNGRADE OR DEFAULT

FASB in FSP AAG INV-a, opined wrap contracts must meet certain conditions qualifying them as "fully benefit responsive." It also mentions if an event has occurred that may affect the realization of full contract value for a particular investment contract, the investment contract shall no longer be considered fully benefit responsive. One particular example FASB gave "a decline in creditworthiness of the contract issuer or wrapper provider" is controversial.

The entire wrapper industry for many years has been made up of large banks and insurance companies rated exclusively AA or better. After 2008 many were downgraded to A. The Stable Value Industry Association industry has consistently argued a default or a material possibility of default would be required to write down a wrap contract. They argue now a rating of A should not be a concern.

Speaking in April at the SVIA's 2006 Spring Seminar in Henderson, Nevada, Steve Kolocotronis, Vice President and Associate General Counsel for Fidelity Investments, cautioned determining whether a particular adverse event makes contract value no longer probable will have to be decided on a case-by-case, facts and circumstances basis. For example, he said, even a decline in an issuer's creditworthiness may not make it probable a fund would not be able to realize full contract value for an investment contract it had issued. [141]

There is no set credit rating in which auditors are required to look at this as an issue. Many in the industry think as long as wrapper ratings stay investment grade, there should be no issues. From the same conference in 2006 Kolocotronis said he can't predict how auditors will deal with such contracts once the new rules take effect or say whether they will require the contracts to be amended or reported at fair value rather than contract value. Brian Gallagher, National Audit Partner for Big Four accounting firm Deloitte & Touche, advised the SVIA audience if stable value managers think they might have a problem qualifying any of their contracts as fully benefit-responsive, they should bring it to the attention of their auditor as early as possible. A solution should be worked out, he said, before reporting deadlines pressure the auditor into a decision.

CAUSES - UNDERPERFORMANCE AND CREDIT DEFAULTS

The stable value industry has typically been conservative in its fixed income investing. There has been a tendency toward durations of around 3 years and overall credit ratings of underlying assets of AA or higher. However stable value managers do compete on crediting rate, so there was a tendency pre-2008 to buy more non-government mortgage and asset backed issues rated AA or AAA. Many of these even AAA securities contained subprime and other underperforming mortgage and asset backed securities. Underperformance results in a loss of market value and a decrease in the market value to book value ratio, the key risk measurement of any stable value portfolio. As the market to book value falls under 97%, wrappers are less likely to be interested in wrapping the portfolio. If the market to book value falls especially under 95%, wrappers may consider getting out of a portfolio via extended termination.

There is a caveat in wrap contracts being that defaulted or impaired securities are generally excluded from wrap coverage. This was primarily designed from a regulatory standpoint to differentiate between stable value wrap contracts and monoline or CDO type coverage of a single credit which require much higher reserves. It is still highly unlikely and could be considered similar to the type of write downs we are currently looking at in money market funds on defaulted securities. Most contracts have credit buckets of 5% which allow any defaults to be absorbed via the crediting rate mechanism. This most likely is a minor issue for a few plans, but is worth monitoring.

CAUSES - WRAPPER CAPACITY

Until the second half of 2008 capacity was not a major issue. [142] And gradually from 2008 to 2012 and into 2015 capacity has become a non- issue. The number of wrappers decreased from the mid teens in the late 90's to 8. When UBS started getting out in 2007 there was little concern. The main overall cause for this decade long decline was the reduction in fees as insurance companies like Prudential, MET, John Hancock, Principal, NY Life and banks like Deutsche gradually exited the business as fees went from mid teens to a bottoming out at 6 to 8 basis points around 2001. However the other wrappers were more than willing to take up the slack until 2008. After 2008 with fees doubling many insurance companies came back in.

The latest data came from an SVIA survey conducted in March 2015. The industry had $77.5 billion in potential new capacity in 2012, $103.5 billion in 2013, $87.8 billion in 2014, and another $79 billion for 2015.[143]

CAUSES – PLAN EVENTS

Wrap providers are willing to guarantee unlimited liquidity for individual withdrawals but are unwilling to allow plan sponsors the right to make mass withdrawals.[144]

The first major plan write down ever occurred at the end of 2008 with Lehman. The industry consensus is Lehman is an isolated event due to the rapid nature of the bankruptcy. This is based on prior bankruptcies like Enron and Polaroid which were wound down in an orderly fashion over a year or more with no negative outcomes.

Plans managers and wrap providers negotiated solutions over time took down rates slightly basically by lowering duration and turning the plan into a money market. However is should be noted Lehman only had a slight negative return for one month December, and participants on an annual basis still remained positive for 2008.

NEGATIVE OUTCOME 1 - PLAN WRITE DOWN

The worse outcome is to lose wrap coverage, and force your stable value fund to be written down immediately. This will be a major accounting issue and require notification of participants. Also because of the implied promise of principal protection it can open the plan up to litigation risk from participants. This hopefully will be a rare perfect storm event like Lehman.

NEGATIVE OUTCOME 2 - EXTENDED TERMINATION

The details of extended termination are specific to each individual wrap contract. Plans and pools can at all times exit a wrap at market value, but unless they replace it with another wrapper this will cause a write down in the fund if the market value is below the book value. The way wrappers can leave a plan without a devastating plan write down is through extended termination. This method amortizes the difference between market and book value by lowering the crediting rate. For example each quarter the crediting rate could drop from 4.5 to 4 to 3.5 to 3 to 2.5 to 2 to 1.5 to 1 to .5 to 0 and could even hold at zero for a few quarters until book value is equal to market value. The mechanism typically starts by setting a maturity date equal to the underlying duration of the portfolio. The duration of the portfolio is lowered as time goes on so with 2 years left the underlying duration is 2. The duration is in the denominator of the crediting rate calculation and as it drops, it more quickly amortizes the difference between market and book value lowering the crediting rate. Also extended termination typically calls for more conservative investment guidelines such as higher credit quality, which could induce selling of assets not beneficial to the plan.

The lower the market to book ratio of a plan or pool is, the more likely wrappers choose extended termination. If one wrapper in a plan chooses extended termination it is far more likely others will choose extended termination as well to avoid being left holding the bag.

Extended termination basically winds your fund down to where market and book values are even and allows you to close the fund or to start over with a fresh stable value fund. The loss in crediting rate is not desirable, but it is a preferable option to losing book value accounting and causing a write down of the plan.

NEGOTIATED OUTCOMES

The most likely scenario for problem contracts will not be loss of coverage or even extended termination, but a negotiated solution. There is a long tradition in stable value industry for wrappers and managers or plans to amend contracts and come up with acceptable compromises for plan participants and the wrappers. Many of these compromises could be seen as partial extended termination in it could lower crediting rates in an attempt to build back up the market to book ratio of the plan.

For example some of the worst stable value contracts we saw at bottom of the market in 2009 had market to book values around 90%. Wrap providers may in some instances agree to allow current investment guidelines but reduce the crediting rate say from 3.5% to a current treasury money market yield of 1% to more quickly get the market to book ratio to at least 95 more quickly.

This would be a way to avoid an "official" extended termination which may cause investment guidelines of lower duration etc. and selling of distressed assets which could lock in losses. It also provides a minimum return for participants with no losses limiting any liability. In most cases there were some tightening of investment guidelines, but for the most part the credit formula was not changed and plans have worked their way back to a healthy state.

As noted before loss in coverage and extended termination were avoided with company meltdowns like Enron and Polaroid through negotiations between wrappers and stable value managers. These negotiated outcomes are designed to be invisible to participants. Compromises in contract terms are the most desirable way to nurse distressed stable value funds back to health.

CONFLICTS AND FIDUCIARY ISSUES

The unique shared experience issues in stable value structure cause potential conflicts especially in collective trust funds. With a stable value pooled fund the Stable Value manager manages for the benefit of the entire pool. For example it may be in the interest of an individual plan to put out of a plan, but since it would have a negative effect on the remaining plans the manager will probably discourage the plan from leaving.

Even in separately managed synthetic accounts there are potentials for conflicts. Instead of compromising as in the example below going from a 3.5% to 1% crediting rate the manager may delay this in fears of their performance record (many based on crediting rates) would suffer. As we have seen in the State Street example they have negotiated cash infusions into plans mostly with the wrappers. There is no one negotiating solely on behalf of the plan, who is to say your plan received enough. Even though investment consultants are on the surface independent, most do not have enough specialized knowledge to get involved in these complicated negotiations, so effectively the managers and wrappers call the shots.

CONCLUSION

Compared to most other asset classes stable value is still relatively safe and stable. Even most of the distressed funds 2009-2012 still outperformed money market funds. However because of the implied promise of principal protection stable value will probably be held to a higher standard in possible litigation.

CHAPTER THIRTEEN

FEES & SPREAD

The U.S. Department of Labor (DOL) issued major fee disclosure guidelines in 2012. I published a white paper entitled *The Big Loophole in the DOL Fee Disclosure Regulations*[145]. My contention is while overt investment management fees are disclosed covert spread in many insurance products is not. This allows a general account product from an insurance company (bragging on making 200 basis points) to show zero fees,[146] while a low cost provider like Vanguard will disclose 53 basis points in fees.

The SEC in their fee disclosures for alternative mutual funds especially long-short equity has included trading spread costs or fees in their total fee calculations to be disclosed, much to the chagrin of the alternative management industry. If the DOL wants to be consistent with the SEC they should have spread of insurance company general account and separate account disclosed as well.

FEES & SPREAD IN GENERAL ACCOUNT & SEPARATE ACCOUNT

I analyzed a statement from Lincoln in 2013 showing the general account stable value or fixed product with 0% in fees. This is misleading when I know they may make as much as 2% or 200 basis points (bps) in spread which is primarily fee like profit[147] I was recently quoted in the Wall Street Journal's Marketwatch *"These excessive profits, even if called spread, act like fees and are used like fees,"* [148]

Insurance companies are manipulating this loopholes for excessive profits. While some may disclose some fees, it tells 25% or less of the story as they make the majority of their profit on the spread. In addition insurance companies continue to pay commissions out of the hidden spread which drive even more sales of these conflicted products.

Currently these higher risk and higher fee bundled products will appear to have lower fees (and higher returns) compared to a diversified low risk low fee product like the Vanguard Stable Value collective trust. In this perverse scenario an advisor with an insurance license can get a kickback in commissions for a product he can claim is DOL compliant with both higher yields and no fees.

The loophole that the insurance companies are using is this. *" The preamble to the participant-level disclosure regulation provides that designated investment alternatives with fixed returns are those that provide a fixed or stated rate of return to the participant, for a stated duration, and with respect to which investment risks are borne by an entity other than the participant (e.g., insurance company). 75 FR 64910"*. [149] I believe insurance companies are twisting and manipulating this rule.

The intent of the exception is to exempt an individual traditional GIC held in a diversified portfolio which functions like a bank CD, 3% rate for 3 years sold in a competitive bidding environment. For example Vanguard in their stable value plan has had in the past a 20% allocation to a diversified basket of traditional GIC's. Traditionally when Vanguard purchased a GIC, the single insurer was limited to 5% of their total holding, and they went to 5 or more insurance companies and get bids to get the highest rate for a GIC of say 3 years. This process eliminates the excessive fees and the diversification eliminates excessive risk. Vanguard discloses a management fee, but does not add any additional fees for the internal spread of insurance company.

Insurance company General Account products currently are usually part of a bundled arrangement. There is no competitive bidding so they essentially set their own rates and their own profits without any disclosure. Historically they have been allowed to vary their rates at the will of the insurance company. However, I think in their attempt to manipulate this loophole they will try to keep rates more constant to appear to fit the exemption which states fixed or stated rate of return. The other qualification for the exemption is a stated maturity or duration and none of the bundled Insurance products I have seen do this.

The insurance industry and its lobbyists have this spin on the loophole. *"For general account products or fixed income products, the Department of Labor (DOL) acknowledges that for a product with a stated rate of return and term, it is not pertinent to have some type of expense ratio related because the real driver of income is the rate being offered"*[150] Again I disagree and think this applies to diversified product in a competitive bidding situation, not in a captive bundled product.

One of the reasons this loophole exists is because the vast majority of the largest and most vocal 401(k) plans abandoned insurance products for their liability risks and excessive hidden fees 10 to 20 years ago. For example the top $3 trillion (68% of assets) in overall 401(k) is large fortune 500 type plans account for less than 1% of the number of total plans and for the most part do not use single entity general account products [151] However the bottom but still huge $1.5 trillion in assets is spread over 650,000 plans (99%) ranging from the small Dr's office to the mid size manufacturer. These plans typically to not have sophisticated staff and also not attracted many lawsuits since plaintiff attorneys prefer bigger targets.

The National Association of Government Defined Contribution Administrators, (NAGDCA the trade group for state and local government defined contribution plans) September 2010 created a brochure with this characterization of general account stable value fee disclosure. *"Due to the fact that the plan sponsor does not own the underlying investments, the portfolio holdings, performance, risk, and management fees are generally not disclosed. This limits the ability of plan sponsors to compare returns with other SVFs [stable-value funds]. It also makes it nearly impossible for plan sponsors to know the fees (which can be increased without disclosure) paid by participants in these funds—a critical component of a fiduciary's responsibility.*[152]

---

1. High hidden stable-value spread fees are subsidizing administrative costs. Revenue from general and separate account stable value options have typically subsidized administration costs, making some participants pay higher administration costs than those in mutual funds, and making products appear competitive in requests for proposal that look at per head administrative costs.

---

2. Fees and commissions are not being fully disclosed. Insurance companies are still fighting not to disclose any spread profits. These excessive profits, even if called spread, act like fees and are used like fees. Commission kickbacks to consultants with insurance licenses are common in plans with general and separate account stable value.

---

3. The structure creates a higher level of fiduciary duty for vendors and risks for plans. Since general and separate account stable-value assets are on the balance sheet of the insurance company, this creates an inherent conflict between the fiduciary care of pension investors and company shareholders. If the firm needed more income they could get it by lowering rates paid to plans since they are in captive non-bid bundled arrangements

Most stable value products (IPG) provided in bundled insurance company products do not fit this exemption in my opinion since its fixed rate is variable and the duration is variable. If the DOL continues to listen to the insurance lobby higher risk and higher fee bundled products will appear to have lower fees (and higher returns) compared to a diversified low risk low fee product like the Vanguard Stable Value collective trust.

SYNTHETIC FEE STRUCTURES

Stable value pricing varies by structures, size and types of clients. Collective Trust Funds typically have higher fee structures. Some public fund clients in competitive bidding may have low fees. The larger the plan, the more likely they have the ability to negotiate lower fees. Since most stable value managers manage both the stable value process and are underlying fixed income managers segregating these fees can also be a challenge.

The number and type of underlying fixed managers can have a bearing on fees. A firm with one underlying Core or Core Plus fixed income manager may be able to negotiate lower fees. Another structure with specialized credit managers, bank loan managers etc. may have higher fees.

We have found in discussions with Stable Value Managers fees for plans over $300 million in stable value assets are many times negotiated. Typically the stated fees do not include wrap fees. Most include both stable value management and bond management. A few break it down to stable value management, sometimes called structure management or roll up management. Mega Plans are charged in basis points with one exception of a Public Plan, where they have negotiated more of a flat consultant like fee.

In a survey I completed for Stable Value Consultants fees averaged 12 basis points for stable value mandates of $300 million and $500 million for mandates over $1 billion it went down to 9 basis points. With current wrap prices around 18-20, all in costs for the largest plans is around 30 basis points.

Morningstar August 2015 article quotes Tony Luna, co-portfolio manager for T. Rowe Price Stable Value Fund. *"As you can imagine, this insurance protection has a price. The costs of the insurance wrappers went up following the financial crisis of 2008 (a period during which the market values of stable-value portfolios were well below book values and some insurers exited the market). From pre-crisis levels of lower than 10 basis points, post-crisis levels reached as high as 25 basis points. "Currently, we're in a trend where 25 used to be the spot, but we're starting to see pressure getting closer to 20 basis points. ... Probably around 20 basis points is what we see in the long term," said Luna.*[153]*"*

CONCLUSION

A large part of the stable value industry does not fully disclose the profits made off pensions. This practice is limited in large 401(k), corporate plans since the plans fear private ERISA litigation. However in mid to small size plans and the entire public 457 plan market and non-profit 403(b) market non-disclosure is a competitive advantage to firms as they can use it to subsidize administrative costs.

CHAPTER FOURTEEN

STABLE VALUE COMEBACK AND STRONG FUTURE

The stable value industry by 2015 can claim a complete comeback from the bottom in 2008. However, it could also be argued stable value participants did not experience any downfall. The only exception was Lehman employees who lost pennies on the dollar in the bankruptcy. Having been involved in Polaroid and other bankruptcies, Lehman could have been managed to be a $0 loss, if it were allowed to play out another year or two under contractual extended termination.

The major disruption in the industry centered in the wrapper community, as many banks exited abruptly in 2008 and 2009. I blame this bank exit on deficient regulatory oversight. The amount of capital a wrapper has to hold for each synthetic GIC was/is the most important risk rule.

However, the bank regulators and state insurance regulators had limited understanding of these instruments, so the regulator of capital defaulted to be the bond rating agencies S&P and Moodys. The bond rating agencies had completely different teams regulating bank derivatives desks and insurance companies, and required insurance companies to carry three times or more capital as banks did. This is 2002-2007 allowed the banks to undercut the business at 4 to 7 basis points.

After 2008 the ratings agencies required insurance companies to double their capital (leading to the higher wrap fees), and the banks, not wanting to put up an adequate level of capital, packed up and left the business. The crisis left strong insurance companies with much higher capital providing a much more sustainable and healthy t market for the long term.

Wrap Capacity is back. In a 2012 P&I Conference call Karl Tourville of Galliard said we have gone from "10 active wrap providers in 2008 to 16 in 2012. The latest data came from an SVIA survey conducted in March 2015. The industry had $77.5 billion in potential new capacity in 2012, $103.5 billion in 2013, $87.8 billion in 2014, and another $79 billion for 2015.[154]

DO PLANS NEED TO DEFEND NOT USING STABLE VALUE?

Because of its superior risk return characteristics, I have written not offering Stable value to participants may be problematic. [155] Money markets continue near zero returns and many bond funds, like those at 401(k) market-leader Pimco, have had performance issues. This is especially problematic for plans over $200 million in assets which have full access to synthetic based stable value.

While some stable value pooled funds for a few years had limited capacity 2014 saw the reopening of two major synthetic-based, well-diversified stable value CIT's. This I think ended much of the shortage hype was pushed by insurance providers who prefer more profitable separate account and general account products to even their own synthetic products. I also think some hype is by the money market industry — and even some firms who provide both stable-value and money-market funds, but make higher profits on money-market funds.

In my 2014 MarketWatch article I made the case. *"What if you as a fiduciary had the choice between two investments with almost the same level of principal and credit risk, but one had superior returns that averaged 200 times higher the last three years, 90 times better over five years, and still over double (over 100%) better averaged over 10 years?"* [156] These are actual numbers as of March 31 2014, comparing the Vanguard Admiral Treasury Money Market Fund to the stable value Vanguard Retirement Savings Trust II.

I concluded the Fiduciary risk of excluding stable value and clinging to higher fee or higher risk fixed-income substitutes continues to rise. I expect this to eventually lead to litigation — especially if money market rates remain near zero.[157]

STABLE VALUE EXCLUDED FROM TARGET DATE FUNDS

While some of the largest and most complex 401(k) plans have included stable value in their custom target date funds, the target date fund industry as a whole has excluded Stable Value, because of its lower fees and higher administrative costs associated with not being available in mutual funds. [158] This is the same reason stable value is excluded often in plans under $200 million.

The stable value industry is trying to remedy this. [159] *"Target-date funds are a freight train running down the tracks,"* said Brian Haendiges, speaking at the 2014 SVIA Spring Seminar." Nick Gage, senior director with Galliard Capital Management, said more than half of his firm's 100-plus stable value separate-account clients—most of them mega defined contribution plans—already offer a professionally managed product or service, such as a suite of target-date funds or managed accounts, that allocates money to stable value. [160]

At the 2014 SVIA Fall Forum Target Date Funds again were in spotlight with Mark Auriemma, LeAnn Bickel, Nick Gage, Susan Graef, and Aruna Hobbs among a group of panelists.[161] There was frustration stable value funds can't be incorporated into retail target-date funds structured as mutual funds and invest only in other mutual funds. Galliard's Gage noted about 15 percent of his firm's separate account clients already offer a custom balanced fund or target-date fund, and sees much potential for Stable Value growth in those larger plans. *"The panelists generally agreed that it would be good if the stable value industry can devise a relatively simple and standard way to manage rebalancing risk within target-date funds so that their product remains palatable to wrap issuers and target-date managers."* [162]

It is helpful to look back at the formation of Target Date funds. I have been a target date skeptic since 2006. In November 2006 I wrote the official DOL letter on behalf of my employer Aegon stating the qualified default options, QDIA, should allow stable value and not be exclusively target date funds.

The Department of Labor by 2005 had already decided up front it wanted to support target date funds by the assumptions they made on stock market returns. The DOL assumed the stock market would return 10.4% annually based on a cherry picked historic 78-year return. Ironically, I point out today it has become fashionable to assert 8% U.S. equity return assumptions are too high in relation to assumptions on a public pension plan. [163]

There have been serious academic papers by Wharton professor Dr. David Babble showing adding stable value to target date funds clearly would add value. [164] Important quotes include: *"...any investor who preferred more wealth to less wealth should have avoided investing in money market funds when SV [stable value] funds were available, irrespective of risk preferences."*[165] ....."*In the mean variance sense, including SV funds in efficient portfolios considerably increases expected return, and SV even predominates over long-term bonds, for levels of risk in the lower two-thirds of the observed monthly return volatility range. In general if the historical returns and volatility can serve as proxies for future expectations, efficient portfolios would not include large stocks, long-term corporate bonds, intermediate-term governmental/credit bonds or money market instruments. Rather, efficient portfolios would be mostly comprised of long-term government bonds, small stocks and SV in proportions that depend on risk tolerance."*[166] Both quotes have strong implications for the construction of custom Target Date Funds including stable value, rather than the off-the-shelf target date funds excluding stable value.

FUTURE

Morningstar in their August 2015 article conclude that Stable-Value Funds has higher yields than cash, with low volatility and principal protection. Although yields have declined in recent years, stable-value funds' yields have exceeded those of money market funds by about 2% annualized since 1990[167]

Stable Value could surpass $1 trillion in assets by the end of the decade. With 2014 assets at $719 billion[168], even with constant market share the explosive growth of the overall 401(k) industry will fuel this growth.

END NOTES

[1] Stable Value Investment Association, 18th Annual Investment Policy Survey Covering Stable Value Assets as of year-end 2013
[2] Unpacking Stable-Value Funds By Karen Wallace | 08-12-15
http://news.morningstar.com/articlenet/article.aspx?id=710877

[3] Stable Value Investment Association's Annual Investment Policy Surveys, 2000-2013
[4] Icifactbook.org

[5] http://www.aon.com/attachments/human-capital-consulting/hist-asset-allocation-chart-may2015.pdf
[6] Chris Tobe, "Stable Value: Asset for All Seasons," *Plan Sponsor* (July 2002)

[7] The Handbook of Stable Value Investments Edited by Frank Fabozzi 1998 Chapter 1 Introduction to Stable Value by John Casell and Karl Tourville

[8] http://en.wikipedia.org/wiki/401%28k%29#cite_note-4
[9] The Handbook of Stable Value Investments Edited by Frank Fabozzi 1998 Chapter 7 pg.94 by Tami Pearse

[10] The Handbook of Stable Value Investments Edited by Frank Fabozzi 1998 Chapter 7 pg.94 by Tami Pearse

[11] The Handbook of Stable Value Investments Edited by Frank Fabozzi 1998 Chapter 1 Introduction to Stable Value by John Casell and Karl Tourville

[12] Why Investors Want Stable Value Funds By Stable Value Investment Association Submitted to the Securities and Exchange Commission February 2004

[13] Unpacking Stable-Value Funds By Karen Wallace | 08-12-15
http://news.morningstar.com/articlenet/article.aspx?id=710877

[14] Why Investors Want Stable Value Funds By Stable Value Investment Association Submitted to the Securities and Exchange Commission February 2004

[15] Why Investors Want Stable Value Funds By Stable Value Investment Association Submitted to the Securities and Exchange Commission February 2004

[16] www.stablevalue.org

[17] Jacquelin Griffin, "Evaluating Wrap Provider Credit Risk in Synthetic GICs," from *The Handbook of Stable Value Investments* edited by Frank J. Fabozzi (1998)

[18] Hakan Saraoglu and Miranda Lam Detzler, "A Sensible Mutual Fund Selection Model," *Financial Analyst Journal* (May/June 2002): 60

[19] Defined Contribution News, "Paul Lipson: CIP, Federal Reserve Employee Benefits System," (June 13, 2004).

[20] Randy Myers, "Advice Providers Get a Grip on Stable Value, "*Stable Times* (First Quarter 2002). Available on the worldwide web at www.stablevalue.org.

[21] Eleanor Laise, " 'Stable' Funds in Your 401(k) May Not Be," Wall Street Journal, March 26, 2009. Available at http://online.wsj.com/article/SB123802645178842781.html

[22] U.S. Asks Judge to Throw Out MetLife 'Too Big to Fail' Suit Andrew Zajac & Ian Katz http://www.bloomberg.com/news/articles/2015-05-08/u-s-asks-judge-to-throw-out-metlife-s-too-big-to-fail-lawsuit

[23] Available at http://stablevalue.org/help-desk/glossary/?letter=all. And www.nagdca.org/documents/StableValueFunds.pdf

[24] www.nagdca.org/documents/StableValueFunds.pdf

[25] Eleanor Laise http://online.wsj.com/article/SB10001424052748703572504575214723494032604.html?mod=WSJ_PersonalFinance_PF2.

[26] www.nagdca.org/documents/StableValueFunds.pdf

[27] GIC ladders can dampen rate hike issues. http://www.fcmstablevalue.com/art3Q14.htm Dave Molin, Peter Bowles, Wayne Gates

[28] Insurance Company General Account DC Investments and the 408(b)(2) Conundrum: Balancing Capital, Liquidity and Transparency By Robert Toth August 3, 2010 http://www.businessofbenefits.com/2010/08/articles/401k-annuitization-1/insurance-company-general-account-dc-investments-and-the-408b2-conundrum-balancing-capital-liquidity-and-transparency/

[29] Eleanor Laise http://online.wsj.com/article/SB10001424052748703572504575214723494032604.html?mod=WSJ_PersonalFinance_PF2

[30] Prudential Says Annuity Fees Would Make Bankers Dance Zachary Tracer Bloomberg March 6, 2013 http://www.bloomberg.com/news/2013-03-06/prudential-says-annuity-fees-would-make-bankers-dance.html

[31] http://www.blueprairiegroup.com/wp-content/uploads/SV-Exec-Summary-Q4-2014.pdf

[32] http://www.blueprairiegroup.com/wp-content/uploads/SV-Exec-Summary-Q4-2014.pdf

[33] Testimony on Stable Value Of Michele Weldon, CPA Chair, AICPA Employee Benefit Plans Expert Panel before the ERISA Advisory Council September 16, 2009

[34] http://www.mercer.com/summary.htm?idContent=1386225 Phil Suess

[35] http://www.nagdca.org/documents/StableValueFunds.pdf

[36] http://www.nagdca.org/documents/StableValueFunds.pdf

[37] Barrons 4/6/09 JACQUELINE DOHERTY http://online.barrons.com/article/SB123880705647288919.html

[38] The Handbook of Stable Value Investments Edited by Frank Fabozzi 1998 Chapter 4 Separate Account GICs by Kevin M. Smith and Sanford E. Koeppel

[39] The Handbook of Stable Value Investments Edited by Frank Fabozzi 1998, Pg.61 Chapter 5 The Evolving History of Insurance Separate Accounts by Patricia E. McWeeney, Kathleen Wong, Michael Vernier, and Rita Bolger

[40] The Handbook of Stable Value Investments Edited by Frank Fabozzi 1998, Pg.61 Chapter 5 The Evolving History of Insurance Separate Accounts by Patricia E. McWeeney, Kathleen Wong, Michael Vernier, and Rita Bolger

[41] Industry publications P&I, etc. 2014

[42] www.stablevalue.org

[43] The Handbook of Stable Value Investments Edited by Frank Fabozzi 1998 Chapter 17 Legal, Regulator, and Accounting Issues by Jonathan Mercier, Alfred A. Turco, Kimberly. J. Smith, W. Mark Smith

[44] The Handbook of Stable Value Investments Edited by Frank Fabozzi 1998 Chapter 17 Legal, Regulator, and Accounting Issues by Jonathan Mercier, Alfred A. Turco, Kimberly. J. Smith, W. Mark Smith

[45] The Handbook of Stable Value Investments Edited by Frank Fabozzi 1998 Chapter 14 Evaluating Wrapper Provider Credit Risk in Synthetic GIC's by Jacqueline Griffin

[46] Sanford Bernstein, "Inside the Synthetic GIC: The Wrapper," (February 1994)

[47] Paul J. Donahue, "The Stable Value Wrap: Insurance Contract or Derivative? Experience Rated or Not?," Newsletter of the Society of Actuaries, Volume 5 Issue 3 (Third Quarter 2001)

[48] Paul J. Donahue, "What AICPA SOP 94-4 Hath Wrought: The Demand Characteristics, Accounting Foundation and Management of Stable Value Funds," *Benefits Quarterly* (First Quarter, 2000).

[49] John Caswell and Karl Tourville, "Managing Synthetic GIC Portfolios," from *The Handbook of Stable Value Investments* edited by Frank J. Fabozzi (1998)

[50] Ibid.

[51] Darryl Brown, Karen Chong-Wulff, and Michael J. Wyatt, "A Plan Sponsor's Perspective on Managing Stable Value Separate Accounts," from *The Handbook of Stable Value Investments* edited by Frank J. Fabozzi (1998)

[52] http://stablevalue.org/news/article/svia-survey-shows-wrap-capacity-continuing-to-grow

[53] Not Your Normal Nest Egg'Collective trusts' are unfamiliar, opaque—and worth a second lookBy ROBERT POWELL March 17, 2013
http://www.wsj.com/articles/SB10001424127887324296604578177291881550144
[54]
http://www.wsj.com/articles/SB10001424127887324296604578177291881550144
[55] Stable Times Third Quarter 2007 • Volume 11 Issue 3 by Chris Tobe Collective Funds Fuel Growth in Stable Value
http://www.stablevalue.org/library/vol11issue3/default.asp

56 AST report.
57 The Handbook of Stable Value Investments Edited by Frank Fabozzi 1998 pg.163 Chapter 9 The Evolution of Stable Value Pooled Funds Kelli Hustad Hueler and Janet Jasin Quarberg
58 https://institutional.vanguard.com/VGApp/iip/site/institutional/investments/productoverview?fundId=0034
59 The Handbook of Stable Value Investments Edited by Frank Fabozzi 1998 Chapter 9 The Evolution of Stable Value Pooled Funds Kelli Hustad Hueler and Janet Jasin Quarberg
60 Blue Prarie
61 http://stablevalue.org/knowledge/management-principles
62 https://www.hueler.com/pooled-participants.asp

63 http://stablevalue.org/news/article/a-consultants-perspective-on-stable-value

64 http://stablevalue.org/news/article/a-consultants-perspective-on-stable-value

65 http://stablevalue.org/news/article/a-consultants-perspective-on-stable-value

66 http://stablevalue.org/news/article/stable-value-the-plan-sponsor-perspective
67 http://stablevalue.org/news/article/stable-value-the-plan-sponsor-perspective

68 Hakan Saraoglu and Miranda Lam Detzler, "A Sensible Mutual Fund Selection Model," *Financial Analyst Journal* (May/June 2002): 60

69 Defined Contribution News, "Paul Lipson: CIP, Federal Reserve Employee Benefits System," (June 13, 2004).

70 Randy Myers, "Advice Providers Get a Grip on Stable Value, "*Stable Times* (First Quarter 2002). Available on the worldwide web at www.stablevalue.org.

71 Victoria M. Paradis, "Assessing Multi-Manager Stable Value Funds," *Stable Times* (Second Quarter 2001)

72 Ibid.

73 Darryl Brown, Karen Chong-Wulff, and Michael J. Wyatt, "A Plan Sponsor's Perspective on Managing Stable Value Separate Accounts," from *The Handbook of Stable Value Investments* edited by Frank J. Fabozzi (1998)
74 Handbook of Stable Value Investments Ron Ryan pg. 11

75 Victoria M. Paradis, "Stable Value Benchmarking," *Stable Times* (Second Quarter 2003)

76 Randy Myers, "Benchmarking Stable Value Manager Performance: The Search for a Solution," *Stable Times* (Third Quarter 2002) Phil Suess

77 Ibid.
78 http://www.plansponsor.com/Barclays_Launches_Stable_Income_Market_Index.aspx October 08, 2010
79 www.galliard.com/LiteratureRetrieve.aspx?ID=66322
80 https://index.barcap.com/Benchmark_Indices/Aggregate/Bond_Indices

81 Ibid.

[82] Victoria M. Paradis, "Challenges of Measuring Performance for Stable Value Funds," *Journal of Performance Measurement* (from the "Reader's Reflections" section) Vol 5 No. 3 (Spring 2001)

[83] Ibid.

[84] The Handbook of Stable Value Investments Edited by Frank Fabozzi 1998 Chapter 10 Stable Value Management by Stephen F. LeLaurin and James P. Guenther

[85] http://www.treasury.gov/resource-center/data-chart-center/interest-rates/Pages/TextView.aspx?data=yield

[86] www.galliard.com/LiteratureRetrieve.aspx?ID=66322

[87] http://www.dol.gov/ebsa/newsroom/pr1003a06.html

[88] http://blog.fraplantools.com/erisa-class-action-filed-jp-morgan-american-century-stable-value-fund/?goback=%2Egde_2128314_member_273386403#%21 Thomas Clark

[89] The Handbook of Stable Value Investments Edited by Frank Fabozzi 1998 Chapter 11 A Plan Sponsors Perspective The Dupont Approach by Daryl Brown, Karen P. Chong-Wulff and Michael J. Wyatt

[90] The Handbook of Stable Value Investments Edited by Frank Fabozzi 1998 Chapter 8 pg. 123 by Ivan Rudolph-Shabinsky and C. Jason Psome

[91] http://www.plansponsor.com/Principal_Real_Estate_Fund_Makes_a_Distribution.aspx Nevin E. Adams | January 30, 2010

[92] http://www.erisafraud.com/Portals/7/documents/PGI_Complaint120409.pdf Keller Rohrback

[93] http://papers.ssrn.com/sol3/papers.cfm?abstract_id=2184534 Measuring Stable Value Risk Structures -- A New Scoring System December 3, 2012

[94] The Consultants Guide to Stable Value C.Tobe Journal of Investment Consulting, Vol. 7, No. 1, Summer 2004
http://papers.ssrn.com/sol3/papers.cfm?abstract_id=577603

[95] *Handbook of Stable Value Investments* ed.Fabozzi 1998. Chapter 14 *Evaluating Wrap Provider Credit Risk in Synthetic GIC's* by Jacqueline Griffin, Chapter 16 Vince Gallo

[96] Available at www.pionline.com/misc/supplements/svf/index.html

[97] Stable Value: Blast to the Past or Too Big to Fail? C.Tobe Benefits Magazine, Volume 48, No. 12, December 2011, pp. 34-38
http://papers.ssrn.com/sol3/papers.cfm?abstract_id=1976453

[98] Eleanor Laise, "'Stable' Funds in Your 401(k) May Not Be," *Wall Street Journal*, March 26, 2009. Available at http://online.wsj.com/article/SB123802645178842781.html.

[99] The Big Loophole in the DOL Fee Disclosure Regulations C. Tobe Oct.12 http://papers.ssrn.com/sol3/papers.cfm?abstract_id=2167341

[100] The Big Loophole in the DOL Fee Disclosure Regulations C. Tobe Oct.12 http://papers.ssrn.com/sol3/papers.cfm?abstract_id=2167341

[101] What Plan Sponsors Should Know About Stable Value Funds (SVF) NAGDCA Nov. 2010 http://www.nagdca.org/documents/StableValueFunds.pdf
[102] 'Stable' Funds Are Looking Shakier April 2010 WSJ by Elenor Laise http://online.wsj.com/article/SB10001424052748703572504575214723494032604.html
[103] Stable Value: Blast to the Past or Too Big to Fail? C.Tobe Benefits Magazine, Volume 48, No. 12, December 2011, pp. 34-38 http://papers.ssrn.com/sol3/papers.cfm?abstract_id=1976453
[104] U.S. Asks Judge to Throw Out MetLife 'Too Big to Fail' Suit Andrew Zajac & Ian Katz http://www.bloomberg.com/news/articles/2015-05-08/u-s-asks-judge-to-throw-out-metlife-s-too-big-to-fail-lawsuit
[105] What ...know about SV http://www.nagdca.org/documents/StableValueFunds.pdf
[106] Mostly Stable Value -BCAP Whitepaper January 2009
[107] The Handbook of Stable Value Investments Edited by Frank Fabozzi 1998 Chapter 8 pg. 123 by Ivan Rudolph-Shabinsky and C. Jason Psome
[108] "Stable value pooled funds: Scenarios for rising rates and cash outflows" https://institutional.vanguard.com/VGApp/iip/site/institutional/researchcommentary/article/InvResStableValuePooled

[109] http://www.groom.com/media/publication/1140_401k_Fee_Cases_Detailed_Chart_4_27_12.pdf
[110] Prudential Says Annuity Fees Would Make Bankers Dance Zachary Tracer Bloomberg March 6, 2013 — http://www.bloomberg.com/news/2013-03-06/prudential-says-annuity-fees-would-make-bankers-dance.html

[111] www.pionline.com/SVwebseminar May 2012
[112] "Stable value pooled funds: Scenarios for rising rates and cash outflows" https://institutional.vanguard.com/VGApp/iip/site/institutional/researchcommentary/article/InvResStableValuePooled

[113] http://www.planadviser.com/MagazineArticle.aspx?id=18294&page=2
[114] Tobe 90 THE JOURNAL OF INVESTMENT CONSULTING P R A C T I C E N O T E S VOL. 7, NO. 1, SUMMER 2004 91

[115] Handbook of Stable Value Investments ed.Fabozzi 1998. Chapter 14 Evaluating Wrap Providor Credit Risk in Synthetic GIC's by Jacqueline Griffin
[116] Stable Value: Blast to the Past or Too Big to Fail? C.Tobe Benefits Magazine, Volume 48, No. 12, December 2011, pp. 34-38 http://papers.ssrn.com/sol3/papers.cfm?abstract_id=1976453
[117] Page 346 Handbook of StableValue Investments Turco et.al
[118] Page 337 Handbook of StableValue Investments Turco et.al
[119] http://www.occ.gov/publications/publications-by-type/comptrollers-handbook/am-cif.pdf

[120] http://stablevalue.org/news/article/stable-value-regulatory-agenda-inches-forward
[121] http://stablevalue.org/news/article/stable-value-regulatory-agenda-inches-forward

[122] Eleanor Laise
http://www.regions.com/virtualDocuments/Kiplingers_Retirement_Report.pdf
[123] http://www.plansponsor.com/uploadedFiles/Plan_Sponsor/news/Rules,_Regs/Lockheedfeecasesettlement.pdf

[124] BREAKING – CIGNA AND PRUDENTIAL SETTLE EXCESSIVE FEE LAWSUIT FOR $35 MILLION JUNE 21, 2013 THOMAS E. CLARK, JR
http://blog.fraplantools.com/cigna-and-prudential-settle-excessive-fee-lawsuit/?goback=%2Egmp_2128314%2Egde_2128314_member_251921108

[125] http://blog.fraplantools.com/cigna-and-prudential-settle-excessive-fee-lawsu it/?goback=%2Egmp_2128314%2Egde_2128314_member_251921108

[126] http://www.bloomberg.com/news/2013-03-06/prudential-says-annuity-fees-would-make-bankers-dance.html

[127] http://www.plansponsor.com/Principal_Real_Estate_Fund_Makes_a_Distributio n.aspx

[128] http://www.erisafraud.com/Portals/7/documents/PGI_Complaint120409.pdf Keller Rohrback

[129] Labor Dept looking into JPMorgan stable value fund | BY JESSICA TOONKEL Sat Jul 21, 2012
http://www.reuters.com/article/2012/07/21/us-labor-jpmorgan-idUSBRE86J1B720120721

[130] JPMorgan stable value fund exiting private mortgages By Jessica Toonkel Tue Apr 3, 2012
http://www.reuters.com/article/2012/04/03/jpmorgan-stablevalue-idUSL2E8EU6J320120403

[131] http://www.reuters.com/article/2012/04/03/jpmorgan-stablevalue-idUSL2E8EU6J320120403

[132] JPMorgan Loses $373 Million Arbitration to American Century Dawn KopeckiChristopher Condon Andrew M Harris
March 23, 2012
http://www.bloomberg.com/news/2012-03-22/jpmorgan-told-to-pay-373-million-in-american-century-funds-case.html

[133] Thomas Clark http://blog.fraplantools.com/erisa-class-action-filed-jp-morgan-american-century-stable-value-fund/?goback=%2Egde_2128314_member_273386403#%21

[134] http://www.bizjournals.com/kansascity/news/2013/05/22/geha-employees-suits-against-jpmorgan.html

[135] Jacquelin Griffin, "Evaluating Wrap Provider Credit Risk in Synthetic GICs," from The Handbook of Stable Value Investments edited by Frank J. Fabozzi (1998)

[136] Unpacking Stable-Value Funds By Karen Wallace | 08-12-15
http://news.morningstar.com/articlenet/article.aspx?id=710877

[137] State Street Corp. adds $610 million to stable value By Christine Williamson Pensions & Investments Jan. 26, 2009

[138] http://www.fastcompany.com/3046630/lessons-learned/7-business-leaders-share-how-they-solved-the-biggest-moral-dilemmas-of-their June 2, 2015 Vivian Giang

[139] "The Stable Value Wrap: Insurance Contract or Derivative? Experience Rated or Not?," Paul J. Donahue, Newsletter of the Society of Actuaries, Volume 5 Issue 3 (Third Quarter 2001)

[140] "What AICPA SOP 94-4 Hath Wrought: The Demand Characteristics, Accounting Foundation and Management of Stable Value Funds," Paul J. Donahue Benefits Quarterly (First Quarter, 2000).

[141] Accounting Issues by Randy Myers Stable Times 3q06

[142] Wrapper Capacity not an Issue by Chris Tobe Stable Times

[143] http://stablevalue.org/news/article/svia-survey-shows-wrap-capacity-continuing-to-grow

[144] The Consultants Guide to Stable Value by Christopher B. Tobe, CFA The Journal of Investment Consulting Vol.7 No. 1 Summer 2004

[145] http://papers.ssrn.com/sol3/papers.cfm?abstract_id=2167341

[146] http://www.bloomberg.com/news/2013-03-06/prudential-says-annuity-fees-would-make-bankers-dance.html

[147] http://www.bloomberg.com/news/2013-03-06/prudential-says-annuity-fees-would-make-bankers-dance.html

[148] _http://www.marketwatch.com/story/these-funds-give-retirement-savers-stabili ty-2012-10-16_

[149] http://www.dol.gov/ebsa/pdf/2012-02262-PI1.pdf pg.29

[150] http://plansponsor.com/Fee_Disclosure_Guidance_Provides_403bs_Comfort.aspx_

[151] http://plansponsor.com/Large_Plans_Account_for_3_Trillion_Dollars_in_DC_Assets.aspx

[152] www.nagdca.org/documents/StableValueFunds.pdf_

[153] Unpacking Stable-Value Funds By Karen Wallace | 08-12-15 http://news.morningstar.com/articlenet/article.aspx?id=710877

[154] http://stablevalue.org/news/article/svia-survey-shows-wrap-capacity-continuing-to-grow

[155] http://www.marketwatch.com/story/are-401ks-without-a-stable-value-option-negligent-2014-04-21

[156] http://www.marketwatch.com/story/are-401ks-without-a-stable-value-option-negligent-2014-04-21
[157] http://www.marketwatch.com/story/are-401ks-without-a-stable-value-option-negligent-2014-04-21
[158] http://www.marketwatch.com/story/target-date-funds-drive-up-401k-fees-2013-09-13
[159] http://stablevalue.org/news/article/stable-value-and-target-date-funds
[160] http://stablevalue.org/news/article/stable-value-and-target-date-funds
[161] http://stablevalue.org/news/article/living-with-target-date-funds
[162] http://stablevalue.org/news/article/living-with-target-date-funds
[163] http://www.marketwatch.com/story/how-much-do-stocks-really-return-2013-02-22
[164] http://www.fcmstablevalue.com/art2Q14.htm Peter Bowles
[165] Stable Value Funds: Performance to Date David F. Babbel The Wharton School, University of Pennsylvania and Charles River Associates Miguel A. Herce Charles River Associates January 1, 2011 http://fic.wharton.upenn.edu/fic/papers/11/11-01.pdf
[166] http://fic.wharton.upenn.edu/fic/papers/11/11-01.pdf
[167] Unpacking Stable-Value Funds By Karen Wallace | 08-12-15 http://news.morningstar.com/articlenet/article.aspx?id=710877
[168] Stable Value Investment Association, 18th Annual Investment Policy Survey Covering Stable Value Assets as of year-end 2013

Made in the USA
Monee, IL
24 January 2020